Savior*
Retirement

*Savior – "one who saves, preserves, or delivers from destruction or danger"

Joe Simonds
Nathan Lee
James Cline
Jason Chaifetz
Franco Devivo

ISBN-10: 1478233524
ISBN-13: 9781478233527

Savior*
Retirement

*Savior – "one who saves, preserves, or delivers from destruction or danger"

Warning! This book contains a Retirement Secret Every Baby Boomer Must Know

Joe Simonds

Nathan Lee

James Cline

Jason Chaifetz

Franco Devivo

Contents

Phase 1: The Retirement Marina. 1

    Introduction: How the Ideal Retirement Plan Is Still Possible,
    Regardless of Market Conditions 6

    About Us. 7

    Why You Need this Guide. 11

Phase 2: Where the Pension Plan Began. 13

    A History of How and Why the Pension Plan Came Into Existence . . 15

    How ERISA Forever Changed Retirement Plan Investing 17

    The Birth of the "SS" 401(k) Plan. 18

    Providing a True Benefit to Loyal Workers in the Past. 21

    Why Yesterday's Way of Doing Things Wouldn't Keep
    Working Tomorrow 24

Phase 3: How Pension Plans Have Evolved into What
          They Are Today 27

    The Difference Between Defined Benefit and Defined
    Contribution Plans–And Why It Matters. 28

Types of Retirement Plans Available Today 32

Why the Newer Way of Doing Things Isn't Working Either 33

Phase 4: The Shift in Retirement Planning Responsibility........ 39

What Happened to Social Security? 40

What Is a Ponzi Scheme? 41

Who Is Really in Charge of Retirement Assets?.................. 44

Avoiding Common Financial Landmines: What's Wrong
with Today's Retirement Planning and How It Can Be Avoided..... 45

Looking Forward for a Solution 50

An Era of Financial Illiteracy 50

Phase 5: The Retirement Secret Revealed 57

A Better Retirement Planning Option........................ 58

Growing Funds Despite the Roller-Coaster Stock Market......... 77

Taking Advantage of Tax-Deferred Growth 78

Accessing a Guaranteed Retirement Income................... 79

Providing Asset Protection 81

Providing an Income that Cannot Be Outlived–
No Matter How Long.. 84

Creating a Comfortable Retirement while Leaving a Legacy
for Future Generations 85

Salvaging Current Retirement Plans: It's Never Too Late
to Change Course 85

The Bottom Line 89

Phase 6: The Safe Retirement Plan For You 97

"The Doctor in Search of a Retirement Diagnosis" 97

"The Engineer's Family" 99

"The Small Business Owner" 101

"The Retiring Corporate Manager" 105

Phase 7: The Truth About AIG 109

Phase 8: The Conclusion 115

Why the Ultimate Goal Is Contractual Lifetime Income 117

Appendix 121

Glossary 131

About The Authors 155

Acknowledgments and Disclaimers

We would like to thank Loren, Natalia, and Shandra for their continued support, patience, and love.

We would also like to thank Susan for all of the great research assistance.

*Savior – "one who saves, preserves, or delivers from destruction or danger"

Many of the greatest books of wisdom have a great deal to say about money, but rarely (if ever) mention the principles of retirement. Today, the word "retirement" has become a mirage for many, and a landmine for many more. The purpose of this book is to give you some retirement principles that will preserve and save you from retirement demise, destruction, and danger. We hope it can be a form of retirement "savior" to you, as it has many others thus far.

Although this book is written by financial professionals, by no means is it written only for financial professionals. When we finally decided to put pen to paper and create a safe money retirement book, we all agreed that it must be easy to read for the college student researching the history of pensions, for the baby boomer looking for clarity on their upcoming retirement, and for the seasoned financial professional hoping to gain a few new tips. We were careful to leave out any financial jargon and have taken great lengths to create a "user friendly" retirement manual.

Furthermore, you will notice the phrase "Wall Street" used many times throughout this book in some unflattering ways. By no means are we saying that everyone on Wall Street is a greedy crook without remorse for his or her fraudulent actions. In fact, we have quite a few close friends on Wall Street who are honest, sincere people. Unfortunately, the honest few on Wall Street have been lost in the mix of unethical and corrupt people "the system" has helped create. It is inevitable that any sector or industry with such vast power and control will become corrupted. With unlimited amounts of money at their disposal, support from the Federal Reserve, a "too-big-to-fail" attitude, lobbyists able to attain anything they want, and absolutely no skin in the game, we have, unknowingly, allowed Wall Street to transform into what it is today.

Moreover, the phrase "Private Pension Plan" discussed in this book in no way is related to, a part of, covered by, or defined as an ERISA Private Pension Plan. As referred to in this book, "Private Pension Plan", is in no way related to or associated with any state, government, or company pension.

Finally, nothing contained in this book should or can be construed as financial advice. This book, in its entirety, is purely educational and is intended to open the eyes of baby boomers, the generation of those born between the years of 1946 and 1964, to a unique retirement income solution. Furthermore, for the many readers who will pursue some of the ideas contained in this book, we urge you to speak with a retirement income specialist before ever making a final decision. This book alone is not enough to help you make a final decision. It is only the first step in educating you and opening your eyes to a new retirement paradigm.

Phase 1: The Retirement Marina

Your toes are in the water as you feel the small waves gently caress the bottom of your tan legs before slowly engulfing the legs of your wooden beach chair. The umbrella above provides just enough shade to prevent you from squinting to read your favorite book. There isn't a cloud in the sky, and the breeze from the ocean delivers the perfect mix to keep you from sweating on this picture-perfect day. You glance over at your spouse and remark about how much fun you both had playing an early round of golf with your neighbors. You cherish the fact that you still have two more hours to enjoy this glorious day before dinner reservations at your favorite fish market. The last forty years of work were grueling, but it has all paid off now. The Retirement Dream is everything it was advertised to be and more.

But suddenly you awake from this dream and enter a harsh reality. The smell of the salt water is gone. The warmth of the sun is gone. The cool breeze is nowhere to be found. Awake, you find yourself wondering why your retirement isn't shaping up the way it was advertised and promised. Your thoughts turn to the fear of running out of money before you run out of time. Will your spouse be OK? Will there be anything left to pass on to the children, or will they be supporting you in your final years? What has happened to the Retirement Dream? Where did things go wrong?

As I write this, much of the news media spotlight is on Europe, our snowballing debt, Social Security running out of money, and the rising health-care costs our nation is facing. However, one of the biggest issues our country will face in the next twenty years lies within our very own retirement system. The Retirement Dream above has slowly turned into a nightmare for countless baby boomers and retirees across the country. The good news is that this retirement book was created to educate you so that you are equipped and prepared to tackle what lies ahead in your own retirement. Moreover, this book contains a retirement secret that only a small percentage of Americans are aware of. This safe money secret is something Wall Street does not want you to know about. It is not a retirement tool taught in our school systems. Yet it is based on the same retirement principles that have worked so well in this country for many decades. It is a secret we consider too incredibly important not to share, considering the number of baby boomers who will be lost without it over the next couple of decades. This secret, which we reveal later in the book, can be life altering. It can change the retirement landscape for your entire family and could care less about how well or how poorly the stock market is performing. In fact, in most cases, it actually gains long-term power as the stock market goes down. It can create a lifetime income stream like your parent's pension while at the same time, protect your principal and lock in your gains each year. Some financial professionals have even dubbed this secret, "The Private Pension Plan". It can be a hedge against inflation and can outperform most safe money vehicles such as CD's and bonds. This plan can even avoid probate and create a legacy for multiple generations upon your death. This secret could be the retirement key you have been looking for all this time.

Many of you reading this might already be asking yourself, "If this is such a great deal for my retirement, why is it still considered to be a secret?" After the past ten years of extreme stock market volatility, thousands of financial professionals' eyes have been opened to this well-kept secret. This fast-growing segment of financial advisors has now begun to highly recommend these private pension plans to their baby boomer and senior clients for a portion of their retirement income. In effect, in 2011, more than $32 billion in assets were placed in these plans. Although that may seem like a large number to most, it pales in comparison to the trillions at risk in 401(k) plans. Furthermore, there has been a complete lack of education for both consumers and financial planners about how these safe money plans actually work. Fortunately, the tide is shifting, and more and more advisors across the country are discovering this retirement secret every day.

In every possible effort for full disclosure, we must also mention that this retirement secret can be damaging if used incorrectly. Like most powerful forces, it can be used for both good and evil. To get the wrong private pension plan for your situation could be costly and painful. It could even hurt your spouse and beneficiaries down the road. In fact, as you do your own research on these plans, you will find some negative press and articles. We are here to tell you that much of it is true. In those cases, the wrong plan was matched up with the wrong person. So it is imperative that you read this book carefully, continue to do your own research, and make sure you talk to a seasoned retirement income specialist before ever purchasing one of these safe money retirement plans that will be revealed in this book.

Now that the disclaimers are all taken care of, humor me for a brief moment and imagine that you are at a private boating marina. And not just any private boating marina. You have been dropped off at the highly anticipated Retirement Marina with a fantastic view of Retirement Island way off in the distance. For as far as your eyes can see, there is pristine blue water like something you have only seen in magazines. The water is so clear you spot porpoises and sea turtles and can even see the beautiful coral reefs full of life on the seafloor. The Retirement Marina was everything you imaged and more. You simply can't wait to get on one of the boats and reach the final destination, Retirement Island.

Your eyes begin to wander away from the amazing array of blues in the water as you begin to look for options to make your journey to the long-awaited Retirement Island. The first thing you notice is a large cruise ship that appears to have left the harbor just a few hours ago. It is already halfway to Retirement Island, and it becomes very clear that you will never make it on that boat. It is a shame too, because the reviews of the ship have been superb. The retirees lucky enough to get on board the four-hundred-foot US *Pension* all seem quite content knowing they will reach the island and maintain considerable income protection for as long as they live.

The next available ship that meets your eye is one right here at the dock, ready to go. You can see the old stenciled letters on the side that read "SS 401(k)." After seeing the massive, indestructible US *Pension*, this ship is quite a disappointment. The SS *401(k)* is half the size with gaping holes in the hull, an engine room filling with water, and a propeller covered with rust and barnacles. It still runs, but you find out that it could be a fifty-fifty shot for you to actually touch the white sand of Retirement Island if you take your chances with the SS *401(k)*. Which ship would you rather be on, given the choice?

Let me summarize. The four-hundred-foot US *Pension* (your parent's pension plan) has already left the harbor, and if you didn't have the opportunity to jump on board, you missed out on an incredible voyage. So what are your options? Well, as we see it, you can either stay aboard the sinking ship—the SS *401(k)*—or look at other options in Retirement Harbor. What I can tell you is that hundreds of thousands of smart Americans have found another boat. It is much smaller, much faster, more reliable, and even gives you the opportunity to drive it yourself if you choose. Unlike both the US *Pension* and the sinking SS *401(k)*, this new boat can turn on a dime, and you can slow it down or speed it up as you please. It isn't a free ride like the US *Pension*, but you will own this boat 100 percent, and you can bequeath it your spouse, your children, or a charity. Also, it comes in a variety of colors, shapes, and sizes to fit your specific tastes and needs.

Continue to visualize your dilemma here. You can see the smokestack from the huge, slow-moving *US Pension Ship* way out in the distance. You can also see that the *"Sinking Ship" 401(k)* is leaving the dock every fifteen minutes with a fifty-fifty shot of making the voyage without taking on water and sinking. And off to the side, you see a perfectly clean dock where a sharp looking crew is filling a spectacular fleet of solid new boats—equipped with the latest GPS equipment, emergency gear, and top-of-the-line technology—with high-octane gas. The sign on the dock says "Welcome Savior Retirement Yachters." We ask you, which option do you want to find out more about?

If you picked the SS *401(k)*, then you might as well liquidate all of your assets and head to Las Vegas to gamble it all away. Why? In essence, that is exactly what you will be doing. Although the Vegas analogy above is used lightheartedly, many Americans are beginning to realize there is some truth to that statement. The closer that baby boomers get to retirement age, the clearer it is that the SS 401(k) is a faulty ship. So don't think for a second that you are alone. This book addresses many of the 401(k) faults, myths, and misleading promises. And no matter how little you have saved or how many bad financial decisions you have made thus far, this book makes clear that it is never too late.

On the other hand, if you picked the *Savior Retirement plan* yacht, then welcome aboard. We are certain that this revelation in retirement planning will excite you just as much as it did us the first time our eyes were opened to its power more than ten years ago. This entire book is dedicated to educating you on the ultimate safe money retirement plan. We will cover the history of pensions, the birth of the 401(k), the shift in retirement planning responsibility, the flaws in our current defined contribution retirement system, and, finally, the secret to creating your own private pension plan. After we reveal this incredible secret, we even dedicate a chapter with real-life examples of an engineer, a doctor, a small business owner, and a retired corporate manager that have personally had their retirement saved by these plans.

Welcome aboard, and we hope you enjoy the ride.

Introduction

How the Ideal Retirement Plan Is Still Possible, Regardless of Market Conditions

As you can probably tell from my introduction, I enjoy boating analogies. As someone that grew up near the water in Florida, I have always been quite passionate about anything that travels on water. I grew up operating everything from canoes, wave runners, bass boats, and flats boats to small yachts and even a fifty-foot dual-prop catamaran I captained around the New Zealand Marlborough Sounds. Simply put: I can't get enough of being on a boat.

Planning for retirement has come a long way over the past two and a half centuries—and even further over just the past few decades. Yesterday's pension plans (aka the US *Pension*)—originally set up, funded, and managed primarily by employers—typically guaranteed workers a fairly comfortable retirement in their golden years without the worry of how to invest their assets during the accumulation phase or the stress of running out of funds in retirement.

Today, however, things have changed dramatically: things such as to whom the responsibility falls for ensuring an individual's retirement plan dollars last at least as long as they do once their working days are done have changed a great deal. You will understand as you read through this book why we christened the 401(k) ship the SS *401(k)*. In this case, the "SS" stands for "Sinking Ship."

About Us

My name is Joe Simonds, and I want to take this opportunity to introduce myself and the rest of the team that helped write this enlightening book. I will also use this opportunity to explain why I believe the secret revealed in this book could have a powerful impact on your retirement, and tell you exactly why we are so enthusiastic about these safe money plans.

To begin, I grew up in an upper-middle-class family in Florida where my family has lived for generations. I mention boating because it is the source of many of my fondest memories. You see, I was fortunate enough to have grandparents with the foresight to purchase a condo on the beautiful beaches of Daytona Beach Shores many decades ago. I can still smell the salt water and fresh fish, and I can envision the excitement as my grandfather, father, and younger brother headed to the marina to watch the boats come in at sunset. If you grew up in a waterfront area, you might recall the thrill of watching the charters unload their daily catch.

We would sometimes have to wait hours in anticipation to see which boat would bring back the largest catch. As a young boy, there was nothing more exhilarating to me than seeing these beautiful boats coming in to port to unload their prized fish for the day.

It was also at this same marina in South Daytona where I had my first lesson in money and retirement. As a young boy at the marina, I wanted nothing more than to be on one of those huge boats. I couldn't understand why my family had a small, used Wellcraft boat when there were so many nice, large sport-fishing yachts all around us. My dad did his best to explain to his young son that you should only buy what you can afford. A simple rule that everyone has heard countless times yet seldom follow in their personal finances. But this rule explained to me why we had a used twenty-four-foot Wellcraft. It was all that Dad could afford. Although it made little sense to me back then, it certainly became clear as time went by.

Years later, this lesson reared its head again. When I turned sixteen, as many of my high school friends were gifted brand new cars and trucks, my parents "highly encouraged" me to get a job so I could buy my own car, even though I was pretty certain they could afford it. And when my friends asked me why I drove an old Jeep, I quickly mimicked my dad's wise saying: "It is all I can afford."

The next financial lesson didn't become clear until years later when the stock market had its first major correction in many years. When you are eighteen and don't truly understand money, most of us assume that if someone drives a new BMW or Mercedes Benz, or if they live in a huge house, that they are rich. The perceived value of glitz and glamour in many cases is just that…perceived. I couldn't understand how so many people in our area of Florida could own all of these nice cars, live in these huge homes, and sail in these luxurious yachts. Were there really that many wealthy people around us? Why didn't my parents have all these nice things? I thought we were doing well?

Warren Buffett coined the popular phrase, "Only when the tide goes out do you discover who's been swimming naked." And that is exactly what happened in the tech crash of 2000. I can vividly recall living in Atlanta and heading home to see my parents in Florida for a long weekend. What I discovered when I returned to my childhood home was that many of the families I had always considered to be "rich" had been forced to sell their businesses, forfeit their nice cars, and downsize their homes when the economy slowed. They had been living on credit and maxed out in debt. With hardly any savings and only a façade of a retirement plan, many of these people will still be working for many years to come. And when the housing crash of 2007 hit Florida, these people weren't just caught "naked" when the tide went out; their clothes were washed miles down the beach. It was the first time I was truly grateful that my parents had been frugal all those years. It finally made complete sense why my dad drove Ford trucks, and we lived in an average home in our middle-class neighborhood— and I finally began to see the world through a different lens.

My wise father helped me open my first brokerage account when I was sixteen. He taught me how to trade stocks, what to look for in regards to P/E ratios, dividends, etc. From day one I was hooked. I knew at that point I wanted to be in the financial services industry. The only question was where I would make my imprint. One of our close family friends was on the board of directors at AG Edwards and ran a large branch for them in central Florida. Knowing my passion for finance and stocks, he graciously gave me a position as an intern for four months before I went back for my last year at Georgia Tech. It was there that I learned from the brokers I assisted that no matter how talented I was, the white-haired Floridians with piles of money would never entrust their millions to a twenty-two-year-old. They told me that to truly make an impact and learn the business, I should work for a large financial services company as a wholesaler. So that was exactly what I did.

A year later, I graduated with highest honors from Georgia Tech with a degree in Business Management and a double minor in both Economics and Finance. I quickly landed a job with a financial wholesale firm in Atlanta and began to spread my wings. It was there that I met some incredible people that remain close friends still today. Moreover, a few of my colleagues from this firm are key members of our current powerful team. It was also there that I began to truly understand the retirement disaster that is forthcoming. Finally, it was also at this firm where I discovered the retirement answer that so many are seeking, though only a small portion of Americans know exist. At first glance, I thought it was too good to be true. But now, after a decade of seeing it alter client's lives and help create a worry free retirement for them, I am confident that a private pension plan is one of the most important pieces of the retirement puzzle.

However, I must point out that this incredible vehicle might not be a fit for you. In fact, if the wrong plan is recommended for your unique situation, it could prove detrimental. But on the other hand, if recommended correctly, it could be one of the most vital tools for fulfilling your retirement dreams. And just as even the nicest yacht in the world will continue running only with constant care and maintenance, these plans will work only if you are willing to give it serious attention.

Finally, I want to come forward and clear up two concerns or questions that many of you reading this might have. First, do not assume that the retirement plan that we reveal is something anyone can get. Second, don't assume that just because you own one of these plans that your retirement is on cruise control. That couldn't be further from the facts. Again, just as a pristine fifty-foot private-pension yacht requires constant upkeep, high-octane gas, and regular maintenance to continue your retirement voyage, these safe retirement plans are no different. This book is also a guide to educate you on what is wrong with our current retirement system. It will reveal the pitfalls and holes in the current 401(k) system that most of us have been led to believe is the answer to a sound retirement. This book is about contractual, lifetime, pension-like income; how to retire in the manner you always dreamed of; and how to actually leave a legacy for your children and grandchildren.

Why You Need this Guide

This guide will give you the history of how and why pension plans were created. It discusses the vast changes that have taken place over the years, such as what today's investor must do in order to create and maintain a retirement plan that keeps them in control even when market conditions aren't. This guide will also attempt to open your eyes to the retirement scams we have all been sold that can't even begin to guarantee lifetime income.

The good news is that regardless of where an investor is today and how much—or how little—time they have until retirement, the methods taught in this book will provide a step-by-step path to creating not just a guaranteed retirement income but an income source that, literally, cannot be outlived.

By utilizing the strategies taught here, no longer will present or future retirees sit helplessly on the sidelines as they watch their hard-earned assets—and their future lifestyle—disappear into oblivion. The Savior Retirement Safe Money plan puts the investor in control today, tomorrow, and long into the future.

Lastly, here are a few highlights on the team of five that wrote this book:

- Collectively, we have completed wholesale transactions and consulted to help reposition more than $2 billion into these retirement plans.

- We have consulted and educated more than four thousand of the nation's leading financial professionals about safe money retirement plans.

- We are the "Safe Money specialists" many of your own financial planners and advisors turn to for information and guidance when working on your retirement plans.

- We have had more than two thousand retirement articles and blog posts published on various websites and in media across the country.

- We have appeared as retirement specialist guests on more than ten different financial radio shows across the country.

- We have appeared in numerous educational retirement videos circulating on the Internet.

- One of our members was a monthly guest on one of the largest financial radio stations in Austin, Texas.

- We have released more than two hundred unique educational videos on retirement and pensions.

- We were the first group in our industry to surpass 1 million views on our educational YouTube channel.

- And, hopefully, soon: Authors of a best-selling book on Savior Retirement Safe Money plans.

Phase 2: Where the Pension Plan Began

When it comes to saving for retirement, many people would likely agree that the recent economic conditions present a great deal of challenges. Given an uncertain economy, record low interest rates, and fresh memories of stock market volatility—and losses—managing and preserving savings can become a real juggling act. It was the recent financial crisis that also revealed many of the gaping holes in the current defined contribution 401(k) retirement system—holes that for many baby boomers, cannot be repaired or replaced; holes that will, most likely, never disappear for those who take the risk of assuming their 401(k) will last as long as they do.

Those who seek to grow their assets are often faced with having to take on large amounts of risk in hopes of achieving a higher return. And, given the shorter time horizon of those approaching retirement, there is often not enough time to recoup from market losses. When you consider today's all-time-low interest rates on safe money alternatives like CDs and bonds, it makes retirement planning all that more difficult.

Therefore, having a properly structured savings portfolio that includes the protection of principal along with the ability to obtain long-term guaranteed income should be a top financial priority. This oftentimes means seeking out a balanced approach to retirement savings and choosing the financial vehicles that can offer varying degrees of both long-term appreciation and an adequate amount of liquidity for the investor. Where in the world, you ask, can you find anything where your principal and interest aren't subject to huge losses?

Overall, for those in the retirement and preretirement stages of investing, of utmost importance should be the ability to turn savings into a lifetime stream of income that allows for a comfortable retirement. This last statement seems obvious, yet so many baby boomers underestimate its importance. With the advances in medicine and increased longevity, *your entire focus should be on contractual lifetime income.* Can you imagine the comfort of knowing you have a guaranteed check being sent to your mailbox every month for the rest of your life? Do you have any friends or family that currently have a six-figure annual pension guaranteed for life? Ask them how stressed out they are about outliving their income. I would be willing to bet that you find they are at utmost peace with their retirement plans. We will be teaching you how to emulate the same kind of plan throughout this book but instead by using a private pension.

Many in the workplace today have the "luxury" of participating in an employer-sponsored retirement plan that allows for long-term savings. Although these plans can provide a way to save for future retirement income needs, the responsibility for ensuring that there are enough funds in the account has, over the years, shifted from the employer to the employee—oftentimes leaving individuals to shoulder the burden of making their own investment choices and living with the results of the returns. So congratulations! The job of a professional pension manager has just been placed on your shoulders. Our plumbers, electricians, dentists, construction workers, and nurses are now forced to juggle their time in portfolio and pension management along with keeping their job, paying bills, and raising a family. Sounds absurd, right? But that is the exact scenario the current 401(k) system has created. You will see many more examples in the upcoming chapter of just how flawed this new defined contribution 401(k) retirement system is. But first, let's discuss the history of the pension plan so you can truly grasp the entire retirement story.

"A History of How and Why the Pension Plan Came Into Existence"

By Nathan Lee

For as long as I can remember, my grandparents have been retired. My grandfather served our country as an aircraft mechanic during World War II. After the war, he took that experience to American Airlines and worked as an airline mechanic with them for thirty-plus years. Once he retired, they began traveling to places like China, South America, and all over our country for the past twenty-some-odd years. They would pack up their GMC conversion van, complete with college stickers from all the grandkids, and drive to wherever they decided to go. Holidays at my grandparents' have always been a time of the year that all the grandkids looked forward to as well. The entire house was decorated and smelled like Christmas. Us grandkids all had sections under the tree dedicated to our gifts. To me, it seemed like they had the perfect life.

As I got older and learned about things like jobs and money, I realized that neither of my grandparents worked anymore, yet they never seemed to worry about money. However, that is not to say they were wealthy. They lived in the same house they built when they were first married, and they only had the old GMC conversion van, but they never seemed to worry about their income. I continued to wonder about this until I too began working and contributing to my own 401(k) and IRA.

I remember sitting on the porch with my grandfather when I asked him for advice about how to allocate my 401(k). He seemed like he was savvy with his money, so I assumed he would have some sage advice about how to invest my first few dollars in my own retirement accounts. The answer I received surprised me and sparked the curiosities that eventually led to my current career and served as a foundation for the research I did for this book. He told me that in addition to his monthly Social Security checks and checks from his military pension, he received the majority of his monthly income from his company pension plan.

My grandfather went on to share with me that he had never invested because he knew that his American Airlines pension would pay for most of what he needed for as long as he and my grandmother were alive. I was amazed that a company could and would continue to pay a former employee for the rest of his or her life. As we continued the conversation, I learned how different his retirement experience had been compared to the one I would most likely have. He put in his time at work, stayed loyal to the company, and upon retirement, he knew exactly how much money he would receive until the end of his days. Here I was contributing to a 401(k), selecting my fund allocations, and hoping that I had chosen well and that the funds would perform positively.

I began looking into the origins of the pension plan in an effort to discover why companies had moved away from them and toward 401(k)s, ESOPs, 403(b)s, and other retirement plans we are so familiar with today.

Although it has incurred many changes over time, the pension plan actually dates back to the early seventeen hundreds when the Presbyterian Church created a "Fund for Pious Uses" to provide needed funds to retired ministers.

It wasn't until 1875, however, that these types of plans came to the United States when the American Express Company created the first US pension plan. Pensions grew a great deal over the following years, due, in large part, to those that were established for the employees of the railroad companies. In fact, the first major employer to start a pension plan was the Baltimore and Ohio Railroad. Here, workers who were at least sixty-five years of age and who had worked a minimum of ten years for the company were allowed to retire and receive benefits that ranged between 20 percent and 35 percent of their preretirement wages.

My grandfather's pension is a direct result of these steps made by the railroad companies. At eighty-seven-years-old he is counting his blessings that American Airlines had such a plan when he was an employee there. I look at him and wonder how I will ever earn and save enough money to fund my retirement for twenty-five, thirty, or more years.

The early nineteen hundreds brought about government-mandated rules for pension plans with the *Revenue Act of 1913*. The legislation was enacted following the passage of the Sixteenth Amendment, which allowed income taxation. It also recognized the tax exempt status of pension trusts.

How ERISA Forever Changed Retirement Plan Investing

One of the most prevalent pieces of retirement plan–related legislation was the *Employee Retirement Income Security Act* (ERISA) passed in 1974. This act required certain disclosure and reporting obligations, as well as minimum standards on retirement plan sponsors in the United States for employee participation, funding, accrual, and vesting. ERISA also established specific fiduciary standards that were applicable to asset managers and retirement plan administrators. It also paved the way for companies to forego offering defined benefit pensions and begin offering 401(k) defined contribution plans.

The Pension Benefit Guaranty Corporation was also established by ERISA, having the primary responsibility of ensuring plan benefits for participants involved in terminated defined benefit plans. ERISA also updated the rules for the *Internal Revenue Codes* for tax qualification of plans, as well as authorizing Individual Retirement Accounts (IRAs) and Employee Stock Ownership Plans (ESOPs). As you will see below, this was the beginning of the end for our nation's beloved pension system.

The Birth of the 401(k) Retirement Plan

One of the most popular retirement plans, the 401(k), came about due to a 1978 congressional provision intended to offer tax payers breaks on deferred income. These plans, named after a section of the *Internal Revenue Code*, allow their participants to invest in a variety of investment vehicles, oftentimes with matching funds contributed from the employer sponsor. It is important to note that the early 1970s were an exceptionally slow time for Wall Street. Back then, the stock market had lost its momentum. Additionally, Wall Street bankers were not perceived in the way they are today as being completely greedy, out-of-control, and relentless in their pursuit of money. Bankers were looked up to and respected, and they earned honest wages. But it was around this time when Wall Street became shrewd and began to influence

Congress through the power of lobbying. Wall Street needed a jolt to get people investing again, and they needed it bad. What they ended up landing was something that probably even the savviest suit on Wall Street never could have dreamed up.

With the help of high-powered lobbyists, in conjunction with ERISA, Wall Street had its foot in the door to what would end up being unimaginable power and control for the next forty years. With the combination of the IRA tax deduction and the move away from pensions to 401(k)s, Wall Street was poised to have insurmountable authority. Because these 401(k)defined contribution plans allow their employee participants to decide on their own investments within the account, the incorporation of the 401(k) plan helped spark a large boom of investments in securities such as individual stocks and mutual funds. Why did this happen? All these securities are controlled by Wall Street bankers who make money whether your 401(k) and IRA go up or down. Not to mention, every single automatic withdrawal from a paycheck into a 401(k) results in a fee that is collected by Wall Street. Think about that for a moment. We are talking about tens of millions of automatic 401(k) withdrawals every single month, year in and year out, by the majority of workers in America. You can probably now start to understand how Wall Street gained so much power and money with this shift in retirement plans.

Before you continue reading, I want to make sure I leave you with a visual of the magnitude of what Wall Street convinced Congress to do here. By denying pensions and encouraging 401(k)s, Wall Street landed what could be described as the biggest sales accomplishment known to man. With the new mandatory injection of 401(k) contributions into the stock market, Wall Street landed a multitrillion (notice that was a "t," not a "b") dollar monopoly deal that will continue to pay hundreds of billions of dollars per year to the fat cats on "The Street" for years to come.

If it helps you to think of it in terms of other careers, here are a few examples of just how big this was for Wall Street.

- If you are in the car business, this deal would be analogous to your dealership getting the exclusive rights to make money on every car sold in America…for years and years.

- If you are in the construction business, this deal would be analogous to your firm winning the bid to build every single new construction job in the country for years out.

- If you are in the citrus business, this deal would be analogous to signing a contract where it is mandatory that your oranges are squeezed into every gallon of orange juice sold in America.

- If you are in the fast food business, this deal would be analogous to closing a deal where every time an American family picked up fast food, you made the profits because you own every single chain in America.

- If you are in the clothing business, this deal would be analogous to making a profit on every pair of pants, shorts, shoes; every shirt; and every dress sold in America.

I hope you can now see just how big this deal was. It created an unfathomable monopoly of sorts that no one can explain. A concept so big that most Americans never even think about it because it seems so inconceivable. Yet when it is pointed out, it becomes obvious. So let me ask you, what usually has to happen in a sales transaction for one party to walk away with complete control, unyielding power, almost unlimited money, and a too-big-to-fail mentality? Someone else (the other party in the transaction) usually has to get screwed.

The powers that be on Wall Street had Congress and big business right where they wanted them. Congress looked like a hero to the average American for giving the public a $1,500 tax deduction for their newly designed IRA. And by relieving businesses of the burden of pensions while also streamlining their payroll systems to have automatic paycheck deductions for every employee in America go directly into a Wall Street vehicle, you can see how this put them in a very dominant position.

Providing a True Benefit to Loyal Workers in the Past

While today's retirement plans require more active participation from employees to ensure an adequate amount of funds, the pension plans of the past provided a number of true benefits to their employee participants. There are a few remaining examples of pension plans today, however, their use is dwindling. One such example is the teacher's pension plan that most states have set up for educators. My parents started as teachers in the mid-1970s, and after thirty-plus years of educating the youth of this country, they finally decided to retire. In fact, they are, most likely, enjoying a cross-country tour on their Harley Davidson motorcycles right now. My parents weren't the best savers, but just like my grandparents, they knew they had their pension plan to support them in retirement.

Again, I think about how having a guaranteed lifetime income has curtailed a lot of the anxiety my parents' have about their retirement compared to other couples their age. Let me give you an example of the income the Teachers Retirement System will provide for my parents during their retirement. The current system pays retiring teachers two-thirds of the *average* of their highest-grossing two years of employment. Let's say a teacher averaged $50,000 over two years and that was the highest income the teacher made during her career. Under the current retirement system, that teacher would earn about $33,333 a year in retirement guaranteed for the rest of her life. And that is without ever saving an additional penny!

Let's assume that for my parents, their average high salary was $150,000 between the two of them. Their combined guaranteed income is two-thirds of that, which equates to almost $100,000 a year for life. Not too bad considering they weren't forced to save additional money or make investment choices for themselves. Just come to work, focus on enriching the lives of America's youth, and your retirement benefits will be guaranteed and well-defined.

When planning my own retirement saving, I started doing the math to figure out how much I need to have saved upon retirement to have a similar income. If I abide by the "4-percent rule" that most financial advisors adhere to, and I want an income for my wife and myself of $100,000 per year, then we would need $2.5 million in retirement savings to achieve that. That is a very daunting figure considering the average working person in their sixties has only $144,000 in their retirement accounts according to Mint.com. I look at that number, $2.5 million, and think to myself, "How can I *possibly* get there?" Well, let's take a mathematical look at what is needed to save that much by my retirement.

I graduated college at the ripe old age of twenty-five and didn't really start contributing to my personal retirement and 401(k) plans until several years after that. Based on the thousands of conversations I have had with friends, colleagues, and advisors, I don't think I am too terribly different from most other Americans in this respect. So let's assume that we contribute to our retirement funds for thirty-seven years, the same amount of time my parents worked as educators. Let's also assume that we contribute the same amount of money every single year we are working—which, in and of itself, can be the biggest challenge because "life" often places unforeseen challenges in our paths. Again, our goal is $2.5 million in retirement funds in thirty-seven years. Finally, let's also assume that our investment choices have yielded an average annualized return of 7 percent during those thirty-seven years.

Guess how much we would have to contribute each and every year for thirty-seven years to reach our goal? (And this is hoping that we can get that 7 percent average return and not hit any major recessions or crashes right before our retirement.) We would need to save $13,603 each year for thirty-seven years, yield an average annualized return of 7 percent, reach a goal of $2.5 million, and take 4 percent of that to give us $100,000 per year during our retirement. All my parents had to do was work hard and provide America's kids with a great foundation for life, and now they don't have to worry about creating retirement income.

For those participating in a defined benefit pension plan, the employer promised to pay participants a specific amount of retirement benefit for life. Because of this, the liability of the pension rested solely with the employer. In fact, 100 percent of the contributions to a defined benefit plan are made by the employer.

The contributions made by an employer to a defined benefit pension plan are determined by a set formula that calculates the necessary amount of contribution in order to meet the benefits paid out to their employees. This means that the decisions on to how to invest funds within a plan are entirely up to the employer.

Although there is a chance of having a shortfall whereby the employer must use other funds to pay the employees' benefits, there is also the chance that there could be a surplus of funds in the account. The job of managing the pension portfolio was performed by highly trained pension specialists and money managers who dedicated their entire career to managing these pensions.

Employees who participate in a defined benefit pension plan are always entitled to the amount of vested accrued benefit earned to date. Should an employee leave a company prior to their retirement, the benefits they earned up until the time of their departure will be frozen and held in a trust for them until they reach retirement age.

In addition, defined benefit pension plans are required to allow vested employees to receive their rightful benefits no later than the sixtieth day after the end of the plan year in which the employee would have been employed for ten years.

In most cases, defined benefit plans will distribute benefits via a life annuity. Using such a vehicle, the employee will receive equal periodic retirement income payments for the remainder of their life.

By using such an annuity, the plan will also allow joint distributions so that a surviving spouse of an employee who passes away may also continue to receive retirement income benefits—usually in the amount of 50 percent of the original annuity income payment.

Why Yesterday's Way of Doing Things Wouldn't Keep Working Tomorrow

Although defined benefit pension plans provide a great number of benefits and guarantees to employee participants, employers have been moving away from them for the past several decades. Two major reasons for the gradual phasing out of defined benefit pension plans are the introduction of ERISA and Wall Street convincing Congress that 401(k) plans would be more beneficial than the already proven pension system.

Another reason for the disappearance of pension plans is that employers are required to contribute every year to fund the predetermined retirement benefits of participating employees—regardless of a company's yearly profit or loss. These plans can, therefore, be a real liability for an employer. Because the funding for a defined benefit pension plan comes from a company's earnings, they can have a direct impact on a business's profits—thus also potentially weakening a company's overall ability to compete in the marketplace. In essence, by phasing out pension plans, companies have taken the burden off of themselves and have left you, the employee, holding the retirement bag.

Many of you are probably wondering what happens if a company that had promised you a lifetime pension goes bankrupt. In many cases—especially when companies fail and must file for bankruptcy—the responsibility for paying out employee benefits becomes the obligation of the federal government, which, in turn, passes the burden on to taxpayers. In some extreme situations, employees who were relying on their employer-funded defined benefit pension plans have had to essentially start over with their retirement savings when they discover their employers failed to fund the plans due to the large expense of doing so.

In light of shrinking corporate profits, Wall Street's dependence and control of the current 401(k) system, increased global competition, and other, more pressing, obligations for companies' funds, most employers today do not offer defined benefit pension plans but, rather, defined contribution retirement plans—and it is expected that over the next few years, employer-sponsored defined benefit pension plans will fade away altogether.

The employer-sponsored defined benefit pension plan like the ones that provide my grandparents and parents guaranteed lifetime income are disappearing for the majority of Americans. Most Americans are now left to their own devices when it comes to their retirement. So how do we create our own private pension plan?

How can we, as individuals, create an income stream in retirement that will last our entire lives? More important, how can we do it in such a way as to allow us to know *exactly* how much money we'll receive 10, 20, or 30-plus years in the future...guaranteed?

Phase 3: How Pension Plans Have Evolved into What They Are Today

Today's retirement plans operate in a very different manner from those of years past—starting with the person ultimately responsible for ensuring enough money exists in the account to fund the retiree's desired future lifestyle.

Years ago, employees who were part of an employer-sponsored pension plan did not have to concern themselves with calculating the amount of funds that regularly needed to be deposited into their retirement accounts or with what types of investment vehicles into which those funds were deposited. Based on a mathematical formula, it was the employer's duty to ensure that when an individual retired from the company, that individual was provided with a set amount of income. Likewise, it was up to that employer to make 100 percent of the funding contributions, as well as to pay out income to retirees throughout the remainder of their life.

The Difference Between Defined Benefit and Defined Contribution Plans–And Why It Matters

Before discussing the types of retirement plans available today, it is important to understand the difference between defined *benefit* and defined *contribution* plans as this makes a big difference in terms of the plan's funding and the benefits received by the plan participant at retirement.

Defined Benefit Plans

"Defined benefit plans," as the name suggests, will pay out a set amount of benefits to the recipient. A defined benefit plan is the old-fashioned pension plan your parents had. The amount of benefit is determined by a specific formula set forth by the plan's sponsor. This formula includes factors such as the employee's salary history and duration of employment. In this type of plan, each individual involved does not have a separate account, but, rather, all funds are kept in a single account from which benefits are paid out to participants upon retirement. These were always managed by a professional, well-educated pension management specialist. It is important to note that these pension specialists were highly trained and highly paid to review and manage these retirement funds every minute the stock market was open.

In a defined benefit plan, all of the investment risk as well as the management of the portfolio are up to the sponsoring company. The plan payouts are dependent, primarily, upon the return of the invested funds in the plan. Therefore, should the investment returns fall short of the company's estimates, the company may be required to dip into earnings or other funds to cover their retirees' benefits.

Defined benefit pension plans can be considered as either funded or unfunded. In the case of a funded plan, the contributions from both the employer and the employees are invested in a trust fund dedicated only to paying out benefits to the company's retirees under a given plan. In a funded defined benefit pension plan, future returns on investments and future benefits to be paid out to retirees are not known in advance. Therefore, there is no guarantee that a specific level of contributions into the plan will actually meet the firm's future obligations. This is why these types of plans are, oftentimes, regularly reviewed by an actuary (an actuary analyzes financial consequences of risk using mathematics, statistics, and financial theory to study future events in the field of insurance and pensions). This review process is referred to as a "plan valuation."

With an unfunded defined benefit plan, no funds are set aside for paying out retirement benefits. Rather, in this type of plan, the benefits paid are funded immediately by the contributions into the plan or by the company's general assets. Unfunded defined benefit plans paid directly out of current funds are used a great deal in most government-related retirement plans, including Social Security.

With regard to employer-sponsored retirement plans, however, the defined benefit plan has been used less and less over the past couple of decades. In 1980, there were approximately 250,000 of these types of plans in existence, but by 2005, there were only 80,000.

This is due, in large part, to more employers adopting the defined contribution plan whereby the responsibility of plan funding and the ultimate retirement benefits are shouldered by the individual plan participants. Once again, the same role that a highly specialized pension manager was fulfilling now falls on the shoulders of the plan participants, whether they have a degree in

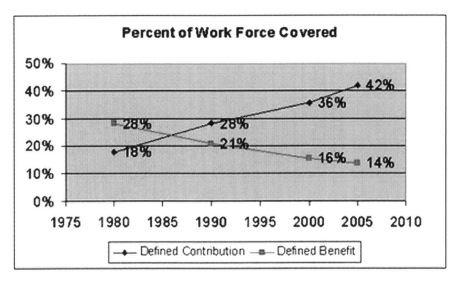

economics or astrology, or even if they have no clue as to how the stock market functions. Nowadays, plan participants are expected to ensure that their retirement plans grow enough to generate an income stream they can't outlive—a job once performed by highly skilled professionals.

Defined Contribution Plans

Although most pension plans of the past were set up in a defined benefit manner, plans used by companies today are considered to be defined contribution plans. The most popular of the defined contribution plans is the 401(k) plan, which has been hotly debated for many years. From the Enron scandal, where employees were allowed to invest their entire plan savings in company stock, to the 2008 financial crash, which caused many Americans to dub their 401(k) a "201(k)," this particular defined contribution plan has many holes.

The Internal Revenue Service (IRS) states that in a defined contribution plan, the employee and/or the employer contribute to the employee's individual account under the plan. The amount in the account at distribution includes the contributions and investment gains or losses, minus any investment and administrative fees. The contributions and earnings are not taxed until distribution. The value of the account will change based on contributions and the value and performance of the investments.. Examples of defined contribution plans include 401(k) plans, 403(b) plans, employee stock ownership plans, and profit-sharing plans.[1] In a defined contribution plan, the benefits accrued are directly attributed to the contributions made to the employee's individual accounts plus any of the gains on those funds and minus any expenses and investment losses. With these types of plans, the funds contributed can come from the employee's salary deferrals (up to a certain annual limit) as well as from employer contributions and/or employer matching contributions. Keep in mind that 100 percent of these contributions go directly into Wall Street's hands. These were some of the same hands that lied and leveraged their way into the biggest financial crash in our country's history.

In 2012, the total amount that can be deferred into a defined contribution plan by an employee is $17,000. However, an employee who is age fifty or over may contribute an additional amount of up to $5,500, which is known as a "catch-up contribution." Overall, the total deferral amount of contributions in 2012 from both the employer and employee is 100 percent of the employee's annual compensation or $50,000, whichever is less.

The employees involved in a defined contribution plan are typically responsible for choosing the types of investment vehicles their account funds will be invested in. In most cases, the sponsoring employer provides a variety of choices such as mutual funds, money market accounts, stocks, and other securities. Oftentimes, the employer's own stock is also an option. Because the funds in

---

[1] http://www.irs.gov/retirement/participant/article/0,,id=211142,00.html

these accounts go in on a pretax basis and grow tax-deferred, these plans are considered to be tax advantaged. Because of this, the IRS has set forth rules governing the withdrawal of the funds. One of the most prevalent rules is that plan participants may not withdraw funds from their accounts until they reach age 59½, otherwise, they will incur a penalty by the IRS of 10 percent on the amount of funds withdrawn. (There are, however, some circumstances that may allow an employee a penalty-free withdrawal of funds, such as a financial hardship or certain medical reasons.)

In defined contribution plans, because the employee has a say in the amount they contribute as well as in how the account funds are invested, it is, essentially, that employee's responsibility to determine how much is in the account at retirement. Of course, when your 401(k) loses 30 percent of its value, there is no one to blame except yourself. So, unlike your parent's pension that was guaranteed and worry free, today's 401(k) plan is looming with land mines that most baby boomers will be trying to avoid for the next 20 years.

Should the account lack the amount of funds needed to provide an adequate retirement income for the employee, the shortfall will need to be made up with other types of income and/or assets such as Social Security and other savings. Considering that our society is dealing with a—for all intents and purposes—bankrupt Social Security system, combined with the lack of savings the average baby boomer has, it is easy to understand why the current system is a ticking economic time bomb.

Types of Retirement Plans Available Today

Today, there is a wide variety of retirement savings plan options available. These can be categorized into employer-sponsored plans, plans for self-employed individuals and/or small business owners, and individual retirement savings plans. In many cases, an individual may be able to participate in more than one option. This part of the chapter was created as an educational building block for anything and everything related to retirement accounts. This can be an ongoing reference for you as you educate yourself on the differences in retirement plans. Keep in mind, the information presented is current as of May 2012 and could change at any time. Make sure to consult a retirement income specialist to get up-to-date information on your specific retirement account.

For many readers, this chapter on the types of retirement plans will be new information, and you will learn quite a bit. For the seasoned financial advisor, much of this should be familiar. However, we are sure that most financial planners will still learn something here. Regardless of your background, we decided to move this part of the chapter to the very end of the book in an easy to read Appendix. Feel free to skip back to the "Appendix" and read up on the scope of employer-sponsored retirement plans. Or you keep on reading along and find out more about the retirement plans available today, at a later date!

Why the Newer Way of Doing Things Isn't Working Either

Although many of the retirement plans available today are considered to have great tax advantages, the truth is that today's retirement plans are not the ideal solution for funding future wealth— or even for relying on a certain amount of income in later years. We hear from so many boomers beaming with pride that they have $1 million dollars in their 401(k) plans. Many of them presume they are millionaires and believe they will have no problems with running out of money. When talking with these confident soon-to-be retirees, we must remind them that their entire retirement plan amount has never been taxed and that either by choice or force, you will pay taxes on all of your qualified money. We also have to mention that if interest rates rise to cover the debt many people have amassed over the past few decades, that $1 million could really be worth only $600,000 to $700,000. And although that is still a nice chunk of money, it is a long way from getting you to the end of retirement without massive stress. Some recent studies have shown that estimated out-of-pocket health-care costs in retirement alone will be more than $250,000 for a couple retiring today!

Regardless of the plan (or plans) chosen to invest funds for the future, there is a common theme that remains: those investing in the market today with a "buy-and-hold" strategy are betting their future income on the assumption that the market will regularly return to new highs. This can be especially detrimental when in the midst of a bear, or downward moving, market.

Yet the question investors must ask themselves is, what if the market doesn't return to previous highs? What if a bear market lasts for 10, 20, or even more years? Unfortunately, in this case, the traditional buy-and-hold investment method would fail miserably—and there is no guarantee that the market will ever go up, down, or sideways at any given time.

Moreover, the buy-and-hold method seems almost obsolete in the "new normal" where super computers do most of the trading based on charts and analysis of when to buy and sell. Our entire mentality has changed from long-term holding to how to make a buck as quickly as possible. It is as if the stock market has transformed from a respectable place for retirement investing to a Vegas casino where the house always win and the individual seldom walks away a winner. Massive leveraging, corruption, and a too-big-to-fail attitude, combined with the financial challenges of globalized markets, have, in many cases, made investing a lose-lose situation for the average American.

Yet the Wall Street casino keeps us coming back for more whether we like it or not. Most of us can't take the money in our 401(k) plans out of the market anyway. And even if we could, where would we take it? Just like the millions who visit Las Vegas every year in hopes of hitting it big, we have been sold a lie that the little guy can make it big in the market by holding on for the long term. However, the past decade has taught us that the only people who made any money in the stock market were the bankers and traders on Wall Street—and they did it at the expense of America's middle class. The worst part is that we still risk most of our retirement funds at the Wall Street casino. We have been told to just be patient, that the stock market will rebound, and that everything will be OK. But unfortunately, it doesn't always work out that way.

A perfect example can be seen in the Nikkei 225, a Japanese stock market index connected to the third-largest economy in the world, just behind the United States and China. This index can be considered as similar to the United States' S&P 500 index, 500 of the top companies in leading industries in the US Economy. Most 401(k) plans have investments that mirror the S&P 500, or invest directly or indirectly into companies represented in the S&P 500.

The Nikkei average hit an all-time high mark on December 29, 1989. This was during the peak of the Japanese asset price bubble, when it reached in intraday high of 38,957.44 points before closing at 39,915.87. More recently, however, the Nikkei 225's high for the entire twenty-first century so far stands at just above 18,000 points—more than 70 percent below its peak in 1989—and as recently as January 2010, it stood at just over 9,300.

Japanese investors who used the buy-and-hold strategy back in 1989 are still waiting for the market to return to its previous highs. In taking a look at the value of $1,000 invested in the Nikkei

225 from December 31, 1989, to December 31, 2009, investors can see that buying and holding is definitely not the way to go. There have been more than a handful of economic analysts who predict the United States will soon enter a deflationary, no-growth period similar to the one Japan has experienced/is experiencing. Is your retirement account prepared for a scenario like this? The safe money retirement plan certainly is.

The value of $1,000 in the Nikkei 225 from 12/31/89 to 12/31/09

Year	End of Year Close	Annual Return	Value of $1,000
1989	38,915.90	NA	$1,000.00
1990	23,848.70	-38.72	$612.83
1991	22,983.80	-3.63	$590.60
1992	16,925.00	-26.36	$434.91
1993	17,417.20	2.91	$447.56
1994	19,723.10	13.24	$506.81
1995	19,868.20	0.74	$510.54
1996	19,361.30	-2.55	$497.52
1997	15,258.70	-21.19	$392.09
1998	13,842.17	-9.28	$355.69
1999	18,934.34	36.79	$486.55
2000	13,785.69	-27.19	$354.24
2001	10,542.60	-23.53	$270.91
2002	8,578.95	-18.63	$220.45
2003	10,676.60	24.45	$274.35
2004	11,488.76	7.61	$295.22
2005	16,111.43	40.24	$414.01
2006	17,225.83	6.92	$442.64
2007	15,307.78	-11.13	$393.36
2008	8,859.56	-42.12	$227.66
2009	10,546.44	19.04	$271.01

Source: *The Retirement Miracle*, by Patrick Kelly

Although there were some positive years in this example, the market provided a negative return overall. In this case, even waiting it out for more than twenty years returned the investor only $271 on a $1,000 investment.

The truth is that those who employ the buy-and-hold strategy could even be subject to unlimited losses, as this technique calls for holding on to stocks—regardless of price signals or negative news regarding the market or the underlying company itself. For instance, despite news and warnings that a company might be preparing to file bankruptcy or is in the midst of a financial upheaval, buy-and-hold investors are still advised to hang on to their shares—even though, at some point, these shares may become worthless and cause investors to lose their entire investment.

At times, investors may also become discouraged with their buy-and-hold strategy and change course. This could be due to having a low risk tolerance during a market downturn or maybe even due to panic about losing funds. This, too, however, is rarely a good idea, as there are often fees involved with moving funds. And there is no guarantee that the new investment will perform any better than the old one. In fact, changing course midstream can be likened to a driver who changes lanes in a heavy traffic jam only to discover that his new lane is now blocked while the lane he just moved out of is moving again!

So what are investors to do—especially those who may still have a decade or more of saving prior to their retirement years? The answer—and the method for how to successfully set up a better retirement planning option—is discussed later in this Safe Money Retirement Plan guide.

Phase 4: The Shift in Retirement Planning Responsibility

As defined benefit pension plans fade away, individuals are left with a much greater responsibility in terms of saving for their future. With this, many are seeking financial solutions that can provide them with not just a steady stream of retirement income but at least some degree of safety, as well. Only a handful of years ago, safety meant a 4 percent certificate of deposit or earning up to 2 percent in your money market account. However, the all-time low interest rates we are currently experiencing dash any hopes of a return from any safe investment vehicle after taxes are taken out and inflation is factored in.

Even the seemingly solid 401(k) plan has met with some degree of uncertainty as investors have come to realize that it is actually their employer and Wall Street bankers who hold most of the control of these plans. In your 401(k) plan, the assets are being chipped away at not only by market conditions but, also, by the significant amount of charges and fees that have been worked into these plans. Rough estimates show that 401(k) plan fees add up to anywhere from $30 billion to $60 billion per year. That equates to

$164 million in fees every single day! Are you starting to see why Wall Street wants us to continue to remain blind to this 401(k) swindle? At $164 million per day, you can understand why this was the biggest sales job of the century.

Coupled with the uncertainty engendered by the roller-coaster stock market has come the understanding that government programs such as Social Security may or may not be solvent when the time comes for needing benefits. Overall, even those who have dutifully saved year in and year out may still be left with very little at the very time they need their savings most. Unlike days gone by, being a long-term, loyal employee no longer yields a gold watch and a guaranteed lifetime pension income. Although it may seem a daunting concept for some, the reality is that today's investor must take responsibility for their own retirement savings—and not just as a glorified pension manager of a dwindling 401(k) plan.

What Happened to Social Security?

Although the Social Security program was never intended to provide 100 percent of a retiree's income in retirement, the funds that are received make up a large staple for many. It is estimated that on average, Social Security replaces approximately 40 percent of an individual's preretirement earnings. With that in mind, not receiving these funds could put a big damper on the retirement lifestyle of many.

Over the past several years, rumors have run rampant that Social Security will run out of funds to pay the benefits owed to millions of Americans—possibly leaving a large number of these retired individuals destitute. ABC News just reported in April 2012 that the Social Security program has enough funds to cover the next 20 years before running out of money.[2] The past few years have been unprecedented in the amount of financial scams in America. Of course, one of the biggest was Bernie Madoff, who bamboozled trusting investors across the country out of billions of dollars. In the end, Madoff was found guilty of the largest Ponzi scheme of all time.

I went to the SEC's (Security and Exchange Commission's) website to see what they had to say about Ponzi schemes, and here is what I found, verbatim:

What Is a Ponzi Scheme?

The Securities and Exchange Commission defines a Ponzi scheme is an investment fraud that involves the payment of purported returns to existing investors from funds contributed by new investors. Ponzi scheme organizers often solicit new investors by promising to invest funds in opportunities claimed to generate high returns with little or no risk. In many Ponzi schemes, the fraudsters focus on attracting new money to make promised payments to earlier-stage investors and to use for personal expenses, instead of engaging in any legitimate investment activity.[3]

Does this not describe the Social Security system exactly? The government takes funds from the younger generation and gives them to the retiring generation in the hopes that they can continue this forever without it blowing up in their face. I guess the original authors of the *Social Security Act* either never thought it would

---

[2] http://abcnews.go.com/blogs/politics/2012/04/social-security-and-medicare-could-run-out-sooner-than-expected/

[3] http://www.sec.gov/answers/ponzi.htm July 4, 2012

actually make it this long or didn't have the foresight to account for a glut of baby boomers retiring at the same time. Either way, the scheme has been brought to light, and many estimates reveal that it has only two decades before it officially implodes. Moreover, the government has had to "dip into" the Social Security fund on multiple occasions for other debt-related issues. How is it that when the government is behind a Ponzi scheme it is called something different? I guess the only good news for Madoff is that when the Social Security scheme finally implodes, it will knock him off the top of the list of the nation's biggest frauds.

The recent US debt ceiling issue has only fueled the fire on these concerns in conjunction with the fact that money in the Social Security trust fund has not been generating much growth. Some experts estimate that under the current system, the Social Security trust fund could run out of money by the year 2033. That is only twenty-one years away. Will you still be alive and relying on those payments then?

One solution that was imposed for keeping the Social Security retirement system solvent was raising the age that individuals are considered to be at "full retirement age." This age, traditionally sixty-five, now grades gradually upward to age sixty-seven, depending on the year of an individual's birth. But even this measure is really only "kicking the can down the road."

Social Security Full Retirement Age

Year of Birth	Minimum Retirement Age for Full Benefits
1937 or before	65
1938	65 + 2 months
1939	65 + 4 months
1940	65 + 6 months
1941	65 + 8 months
1942	65 + 10 months
1943–1954	66
1955	66 + 2 months
1956	66 + 4 months
1957	66 + 6 months
1958	66 + 8 months
1959	66 + 10 months
1960 or after	67

Source: SSA *Publication 05-10024, August 2011*

Another potential solution is for individuals to invest their own funds, earmarked for Social Security, into potentially higher-yielding stocks. However, this fix has a high probability of backfiring—especially in light of the unpredictable market. Not to mention, who would manage the portfolio? It is already clear that the average American cannot actively manage his or her retirement investments. In 2008 alone, 401(k) plans and individual retirement accounts lost $2.8 trillion in value. To make matters worse, thirty-six percent of American workers age 55 to 64 say they have less than $25,000 in retirement savings, according to a survey by the Employee Benefit Research Institute. Imposing a second obligation to have them manage their own Social Security investment would, no doubt, be an even bigger nightmare down the road. In fact, by doing so, those who are counting on these funds could actually end up in a similar situation as having their 401(k) plan and other retirement funds invested in the stock market—at risk for a tremendous loss of retirement funds that may or may not ever be regained.

Who is *Really* in Charge of Retirement Assets?

All investments carry some degree of risk along with potential reward. Over the years, a number of "self-directed" retirement savings plans have come into existence allowing investors to choose the underlying financial vehicles in which to invest their funds. In taking a closer look at the self-directed plans, however, it is plain to see that many of them actually impose a large number of rules, restrictions, and even penalties in certain situations. And while today's 401(k) plans may allow investors a choice of where to invest their funds, the options are often limited to just a few mutual funds and stocks picked by the employer. In many cases, the employer doesn't even know if the available funds are any good at all. In addition, these accounts—as well as Individual Retirement Accounts (IRAs)—are unusually burdened with maximum contribution limits, a minimum age at which withdrawals can be made, and, in most cases, an underlying dependence on the performance of the market.

Government programs such as Social Security are similar in that those who have been faithfully paying into the system truly have no control over where those dollars go—or even *if* those dollars will be there for them in retirement. I, for one, am not counting on seeing a single dime of the money I was forced to contribute to Social Security.

So the question remains, who really is in charge of an investor's future retirement income? The answer going forward is that it has to be the individual investor that takes the reins on their future. The secret that will be revealed in the coming chapters should be one of your first steps in taking control of your retirement destiny. And just like anything at which you want to be successful, it all begins with proper education.

Avoiding Common Financial Landmines–What's Wrong with Today's Retirement Planning and How It Can Be Avoided

Many of today's investors—and especially those who are nearing retirement and/or have suffered significant market losses over the past few years—are now approaching the concept of saving for the future with a very different view than was taken just a decade ago.

Gone are the days when nearly any stock investment was practically guaranteed to provide investors a nice high return, and even the investment options considered to be safer, such as bonds and CDs, are not netting investors nearly what they will need in order to live a comfortable retirement lifestyle. And you can no longer count on your home to provide a solid equity increase every year. What was always considered the American dream—to own a home and see it appreciate—turned into an ugly nightmare after greed and corruption were allowed to enter. It almost seems that everything we have been taught our entire lives that is supposed to be a solid investment has turned out to be a financial fluke.

Yet, while a large part of investing has to do with the market—which, essentially, cannot be controlled—there are other factors investors can plan for or, at the very least, avoid to reduce or eliminate potential landmines to future wealth. And although some of these landmines may seem obvious, there are still a great many investors who fall victim to them—and these individuals often realize their mistakes when it is already too late.

Some of the most common landmines related to finance and investing include over-diversifying, not taking time horizon into consideration, trading too frequently, making decisions based on fear, no exit strategy, not planning for an early death, not planning for a disability, not planning for long term care costs, and investment scams:

- **Over-diversifying** – While most investors understand it is not a good idea to put all of their eggs in one basket, there are some who may take the concept of diversification too far and do themselves more harm than good in the process.

Depending on the amount of total funds an investor has, it is best to consider a number of different types of investments yet not take the process so far that each investment has only a slight impact on the overall portfolio. In addition, by making numerous unnecessary investments, the associated brokerage commissions and other transaction costs and fees may end up exceeding the amount of profit or return gained on each of the positively performing investments.

An index-related investment may better serve those investors prone to the "dig-a-hundred-different-holes-and-put-a-dollar-in-each" method, as by the very nature of such vehicles, there are many different components involved but with much lower associated fees and, oftentimes, much less overall risk.

- **Not taking time horizon into consideration** – Regardless of an investor's age, it is the actual investment time horizon that should be taken into consideration with each and every investment made. For example, those who will need their funds within a short time frame such as one or two years should not invest their funds in stocks or equity-based mutual funds, as these have the potential to produce a negative return and are not likely to regain their losses within a short time frame. Likewise, for those investors who have an investment time horizon of ten or more years, CDs and bonds should likely be avoided, as their returns are typically lower than what can be achieved in more growth-oriented alternatives.

- **Trading too frequently** – Although there are professional traders who make their living timing the market and initiating frequent trades, for most investors, this is not the way to make a fortune or even a positive return in most cases. In today's trading world, the work is done by supercomputers that can disseminate information and execute trades faster than any team of humans ever could manually. By the time information about a certain investment reaches the average American, it is usually way too late to do anything. Also, frequent trading does not allow equity investors to truly take part in the rising value of a good stock. This is also another area where broker-age commissions and other related transaction fees can really eat into the potential profit of an investment.

- **Making investment decisions based on fear** – One of the absolute costliest mistakes investors can make is that of investing based on fear. Many investors will conduct their research and select good investments, yet if the market dips down even slightly, they hurry to sell their stock for fear of losing their money. This is what Wall Street commonly refers to as "dumb money"—always selling or buying at the absolute wrong time.

In this case, it is imperative to stick to the basic theory of "buy low, sell high"—but not with every bump in the market. True return is made when investors are willing to ride out the storms with good investments. Investors' patience is oftentimes rewarded with profit.

- **Not having an exit strategy** – For those who are business owners, one of the biggest financial landmines can be not having an exit strategy. This concept can mean different things to different people, including retirement or the sale of a business.

- **Not planning for an early death** – Although most people do not like to think about it, the probability of an early or unexpected death still needs to be planned for. If not planned for, an early death could spell financial disaster for the loved ones left behind.

Certainly, some of the best ways to plan for this include purchasing adequate life insurance coverage, creating an emergency fund for loved ones, and ensuring that health-insurance coverage is substantial enough to pay for potential end-of-life or emergency medical procedures. Good, solid life insurance protection can help loved ones pay off debts such as a mortgage, auto loan, and credit card balances. Life insurance funds can also provide an income for either the short or long term, depending on the survivors' needs.

- **Not planning for disability** – When asked what they believe their most valuable asset to be, many individuals will reply that it is their home, their business, or their retirement savings. However, the truth is that a person's most important asset is his or her ability to earn an income— because without it, the other assets would be impossible to obtain. Therefore, planning for income replacement due to a severe illness or disability is essential for avoiding the financial landmine of having no income with which to pay living expenses. The best way to do so entails the purchase of a good, solid disability insurance policy.

Oftentimes, these types of plans are offered through employers. However, it is important to be sure that an employer-sponsored disability insurance plan covers more than just a short-term episode. If this is the case, then obtaining an individual long-term disability plan should also be considered.

- **Not planning for long-term care costs** – Similar to death and disability, the discussion of long-term care needs is not likely to be at the top of most people's retirement planning lists. Yet the reality of a potential need for care—as well as the associated costs—is higher than most people think. In fact, once an individual reaches the age of sixty-five, there is an approximately 1-in-3 chance that they will need long-term care for at least some period of time. And, for those who will require this type of care, the average need is between two and three years.

With the average annual cost of a semiprivate room in a skilled nursing facility near $80,000, this is a potential financial landmine that should definitely not be overlooked—especially by those approaching retirement age and who do not have assets allocated for paying these types of costs.

- **Investment scams** – Although it's unfortunate, the world is full of individuals and businesses designed to do one thing: fleece people of their money. And the financial industry seems to be full of these "opportunities." There are several things that can be done, however, to avoid the landmine of financial scams.

First, if the deal sounds too good to be true, it probably is. Therefore, it should likely be avoided at all costs. Another defense is that of researching the Internet for any complaints about the company or investment being considered. Two of the best websites for this are the Better Business Bureau's (www.bbb.org) and the SEC's (www.sec.gov). In addition, if the company in question is offering insurance or securities, research may be conducted on each state's individual Department of Insurance website as well as on the FINRA (Financial Industry Regulatory Authority) website to ensure the company or individual offering the deal is a legitimate broker or agent who is licensed and qualified to provide such products or services.

Looking Forward for a Solution

For those who have a long-term objective of building a guaranteed source of lifetime income, saving for a specific retirement goal, and/or leaving a legacy for their loved ones, there is a solution that will meet their retirement income needs while also providing tax advantages and reducing a great deal of uncertainty going forward. As we mentioned at the beginning of the book, this retirement secret can be life altering if used correctly.

And while many of today's current retirement savings plans offer little control to the investor, the twenty-first-century pension, our Safe Money Retirement Plan, puts the control back where it belongs: in the hands of the individual investor.

"An Era of Financial Illiteracy: Where Has Financial Education Gone?"
By Jason Chaifetz

I have had the luxury of working in the retirement product business for eight years. Most people in my age group have not had that opportunity. My friends are constantly asking me questions that seem ridiculous at this point in our lives. I'll give you a simple example: Many of my friends have little or no retirement savings and many more carry credit card debt even if they can afford to pay it off. I know they understand the simple math that if they are paying 15 percent interest on their credit card debt that the smartest decision would be to pay off that debt unless they could invest that same money guaranteed at more than 15 percent. The issue is that these lessons were never taught. I digress, but the point is that as we shift the responsibility of retirement fund planning and growing from the employer to the employee, we need to incentivize financial education that can help these individuals. If we don't educate people about financial matters, the results will be catastrophic, as we will have generations of people who are completely unprepared for retirement, who are financially illiterate, and who are in need of even more retirement money from a dying Social Security system.

I had the great fortune of spending a year in Switzerland exploring the beautiful country, meeting some great people, and getting away from the hustle and bustle of everyday life here in America. I spent a large amount of time with a girl my age that I met while working in California. She brought me in like family, and it was there that I really began to learn about the Swiss culture and their retirement system. Around the time I was there, her parents were reaching retirement age. I would consider her parents to be upper-middle class by American standards. Although the Swiss are known for their secrecy, I did have a few conversations on how their retirement system works. The Swiss have a "four-legged stool" system and are forced to pay into three of the "legs," with the fourth being optional. To stay on point, I won't go into fine details, but what amazed me was that her parents were going to be getting a large percentage (around 75 percent) of their salary for the rest of their life in a pension-type payout. I remember trying to do the math on the size of a portfolio that I would have to achieve to have this same income stream. The numbers were mind-boggling to say the least. Witnessing the stress-free nature of the pension payout system firsthand made me long for the days of yore in this country.

In Australia, citizens can put up to $100,000 into their "Super" (short for superannuation) annually. This is on top of the 12 percent or more of their salary that their employers put in on their behalf. This is an account that the citizen can invest as he or she sees fit. What's amazing about these accounts is that not only are contributions tax deductible but retirement withdrawals are tax free! Basically, these accounts are the best of both the Traditional and Roth IRA worlds. I find it amazing that a country that offers socialized medicine also offers such a fantastic retirement program to its citizens. The truth is that even with these tax-favorable accounts, you still need a safe place to put a portion of your money that it is not susceptible to financial crisis, recessions, or depressions.

We cannot control the taxes in this country, and for all of our system's shortcomings, I am proud to be a citizen of the greatest country on Earth. The system is already in place—we just have to find a way to work within the parameters. The good news is that there are products that can help not only us as investors but, also, the entire system. If we can remove dependence on the system, there will be more money for other programs or even a reduction in our country's deficit.

I grew up in a wealthy suburb of Atlanta, Georgia, known as East Cobb. The area had a reputation for being full of pretentious people that had all been born with silver spoons in their mouths. In fact, we were frequently referred to as "East Cobb Snobs." I can, however, assure you that this was not the case. If it was, I am still waiting for my silver spoon. In East Cobb, you have the "million-aire next door" right next to the "keeping-up-with-Joneses" types. But for every millionaire next door, there were at least ten keeping-up-with-the-Joneses households. When kids in East Cobb turn sixteen, they all get muscle cars, big trucks, or jeeps given to them by their parents. They believe that they have truly rich parents and that they will lead a privileged life. Little do they know that nine out of ten of their parents have been digging huge ditches of debt to maintain the appearance of being wealthy. It's more likely that these kids will be taking care of their parents financially, assuming they are able to.

We live in a country of consumerism—a country where material objects are overvalued. Our society is substantially mortgaging its future both on the government level and the personal level just to have things now. We are in a world of immediate gratification. This further affects our retirement picture because we are so focused on having that new iPad, TV, or automobile that we are willing to forego adding to our retirement accounts for the opportunity to splurge. This creates a cultural cycle of spenders versus savers. Now, in the days of employer-assisted retirement preparation, such people were saved from themselves. This further strengthens my point that we need more education on not just money in general but on retirement money in particular.

The question becomes, does the United States government really want its people to be financially prepared for retirement? Based on my experience, I believe the answer is "No". Let's think this through for a second. If no one (or very few people) needed Social Security, the government has less control over the people. This same idea carries over to welfare and Medicare/Medicaid as well. If we did not need these services, then the money these services provide could not tempt us. This would lend itself to a smaller government, a more efficient government, and a government that has less power over our lives. Likewise, if all Americans were savers and had robust retirement plans, our society that thrives on consumption would also cease to exist. A society of savers vs spenders (the opposite of reality today in America) would almost make the government obsolete compared to its massive structure today.

Also, in an economy already so dependent on consumerism, if taught fiscal responsibility, there would be a reduction in spending that could, possibly, spiral the entire economy into a recession or, worse, a depression. This is especially true as we try to dig our way out of the hole the housing and financial crises left us in.

In a world where people are ill-prepared for their golden years, we are even more susceptible to swings in the market caused by anything from economic recessions to terrorist attacks. We need a safe place where we can put our money but that still allows for the opportunity for strong, guaranteed growth for retirement. Let's face it, many of us are going to be stretching every dollar we have as we get to our retirement years.

One of the biggest advantages of the pension plans of days past was the opportunity to have an income stream that you (and your spouse) could not outlive. If you have ever known someone with a pension, you know that the benefits of a lifetime income make life a lot less stressful during retirement. Even if you are a saver or investor and have socked away a nest egg for retirement, you now have the task of spending down your assets in your golden years. This sounds great, but how do you know how much to take out so that your money will continue through all your years of retirement? How do you make sure your income increases with inflation? What if the stock market makes a significant correction during your twilight years? Who do you turn to for these answers? The biggest fear among retirees right now—even more than death—is outliving their savings.

If you have a retirement nest egg, chances are you already work with a broker or advisor. The issue, then, becomes how different the deccumulation phase can be from the accumulation phase. "Accumulation" refers to your the years from 20 to 60 years old where most American's work, try to save as much as they can, raise and educate children, etc. It is in this phase that your utmost concern is getting a return on your investment and ensuring that you have enough to last you for the second half of your life. "Deccumulation" refers to the second half of your life where your ultimate goal is preservation and lifetime income. The double digit annual returns would be gladly exchanged for safety and security of a contractual guarantee. The objective of deccumulation is to create lasting income off of your accumulated retirement savings that will always outlast you. You or your broker may have been an expert at dollar-cost averaging your account over the past thirty years, but spending down the asset is an entirely different animal. If you're working with a broker or financial advisor that concentrates on growth, I strongly recommend that you look for an advisor that deals specifically with retirement income. In many ways, financial advisors are like doctors, and certain advisors specialize in certain areas of money. Just as you would not go see an ear, nose, and throat specialist for a torn ACL, you should not work with an advisor that concentrates on accumulation when it is time to prepare for your income in retirement.

We touched earlier on the lack of education offered on the subject of money, investing, and budgeting. We also touched on the culture of consumption in this country and the need to have material things. We discussed the shift of responsibility of retirement from the employer to the employee. If we agree that having a guaranteed check in the mailbox every month just like we had in our working years is a good thing, and I hope we do, then we just need to find a way to accomplish this feat. We need a way to get back to the pension plan system.

The question becomes, is there a way to duplicate the pension plan system? Is there a way to privatize the pension plan? If corporations could do it, why can't individuals? And if the product, system, or plan existed, how could you get the word out to the people?

Phase 5: The Safe Money "Savior" Retirement Plan

"The Secret Revealed"

Over the past few years, the financial markets have gone through a myriad of ups and downs, leaving most investors on edge—especially those approaching their retirement years. This can be a tragedy that brings to light one of the biggest fears an investor faces: running out of money during retirement. A study by Allianz titled *Reclaiming the Future* revealed that 61 percent of baby boomers fear outliving their money in retirement over death.

Although many have seen their hard earned savings disappear and are leery about jumping back into the "fire" with what they have left, there are options available that can help investors achieve their financial goals while, also, offering peace of mind for concerns such as outliving retirement assets and keeping retirement income on par with inflation.

A Better Retirement Planning Option

Today, investors have limited options available to them that can put them back in the driver's seat. So what is this incredible retirement secret that we consider the "best of all worlds" for baby boomers? The secret is the fixed index annuity, also known as the Safe Money Retirement plan, and in some financial professional circles, also referred to as the private pension plan. With this financial vehicle, investors can receive a lifetime income that starts either immediately upon a lump sum deposit or at some time in the future. It is capable of delivering contractual lifetime income at almost any date in the future and can even be stopped and started at the control of the owner. And this is not your parent's annuity that loses all value upon death. These twenty-first century private pension plans come equipped with death benefits, nursing home benefits, and even long-term care benefits in some cases.

Moreover, these financial products can offer their holders a unique combination of benefits that can provide tax-deferred growth of funds within the account, the potential for a nice return based on indexed interest, and an amount of protection for the investor's retirement assets and income. These fixed indexed annuities have minimum guarantees built in, and if you play by the rules, you can never lose your principal or any gains you have earned. This chapter will outline the crucial pieces of a fixed index annuity such as annual reset and the extremely powerful guaranteed lifetime income benefit riders that contractually deliver annual deferred gains and eventual lifetime income.

The fixed index annuity can offer their holders interest earnings potential linked to a market index, yet it will completely avoid market downturns. This savings vehicle is very appealing to those who understand the long-term benefit of investing in equities but are not comfortable with the volatility and potential losses that are a common part of investing. Most of these fixed indexed annuities contain an "annual reset" feature that locks in your gains each year while crediting the account with a zero in years that your index goes negative. Where these annuities really gain more momentum is when any positive return is automatically added on top of your prior locked in gains.

Index annuity owners fortunate enough to have had their retirement money in one of these fixed index annuities prior to 2008 have done extremely well. Consider that in 2008, these annuity owners did not lose a penny. And instead of seeing their retirement savings drop 25 percent, 30 percent, or even 50 percent in some cases, they simply received a zero for the year (which, although not a gain, is much better than negative). As the market recovered in 2010, these annuity owners were eligible to participate in some of these gains without having to make up for any losses like the rest of us. You will see over the following few pages how powerful this annual reset feature can be. Check out the chart below from American Equity on "The 'Real Benefits' of Indexed Annuities with Annual Reset Design."

These products were created with the purpose of offering a return that falls somewhere between basic savings instruments such as CDs/bonds and stock market gains. With typically higher returns than other conservative options, coupled with the safety of principal they can offer, fixed index annuities have become a very popular choice—especially for retirees and baby boomers approaching retirement.

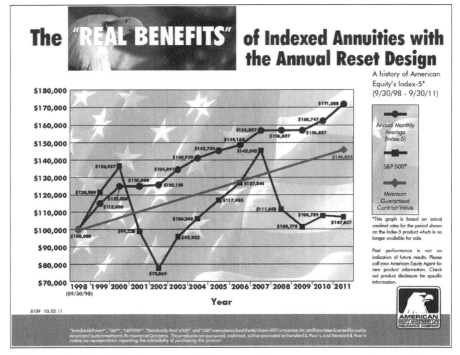

Source: American Equity Investment Life Insurance Company – www.american-equity.com

How Fixed Index Annuities Work

A fixed index annuity, or FIA, is, technically, an insurance contract between an investor and the offering insurance company. In exchange for a premium payment—either one lump sum or periodic deposits—the insurance company provides the investor with a stream of income. And don't think of this as the annuity you learned about in Economics 101 where you invest money with a company and they start paying you a lifetime income right away in hopes that you pass away quickly. In fact, it couldn't be farther from the truth with these fixed index annuities. These vehicles are designed to be held in deferral for as long as twenty years in some cases before you turn on an income stream. There are also some that are created for the consumer that needs income right now. Whatever your situation, these annuities are designed to leave your spouse or beneficiary with a legacy if you haven't already maximized your benefits. So an early death doesn't spell doom for the annuity or your beneficiaries.

Annuities come in many shapes and sizes but can usually be lumped into three different groups: Fixed Annuities, Income Annuities, and Variable Annuities. Fixed annuities encompass multi-year guarantee annuities, adjustable fixed rate annuities, and fixed indexed annuities. Income Annuities are also known as single premium immediate annuities and will always produce some sort of contractual income. Finally, variable annuities are securities that contain all of the features of annuities with more risk (and thus more potential upside), as they contain investment options such as mutual funds, bonds, etc.

Similar to other types of annuities, a fixed index annuity can be either immediate or deferred, meaning that benefits may be paid out to its holder either immediately (or very soon after) an initial lump sum deposit is made, or deposits can be made over time with benefits also being paid out over a series of years—or even for the remainder of the recipient's lifetime.

What makes these products different from regular fixed annuities is that the growth in the account is based on the performance of an underlying index—and the value of this index is tied to a stock market or other type of index. Some of the more common indices tracked by a fixed index annuity are the Standard & Poor's (S&P) 500 and the Dow Jones Industrial Average (DJIA).

It is important to note that because the holder of an FIA does not actually invest in the underlying market, fixed index annuities are not considered to be securities. Therefore, these products are not required to be registered under the *Securities Act of 1933* and are sold by registered insurance companies as an insurance product.

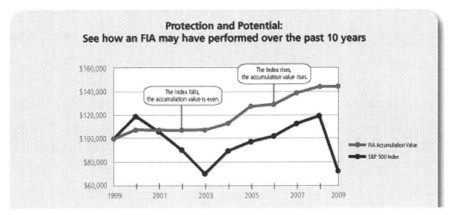

These fixed index annuities are also different from their fixed annuity counterparts because of the diverse amount of lifetime income riders that can be attached to them. These income riders, commonly known as GLIBs (Guaranteed Lifetime Income Benefits), come in many shapes and sizes with one common objective: to contractually guarantee a flexible income stream for the remainder of your life. But keep in mind, the powerful FIA does not come standard with any riders. Riders are add-ons that, in most cases, you would pay a small annual fee for. Many consumers buy these FIAs as a standalone for their safety and ability to outperform other safe-money alternatives. And unlike variable annuities, these fixed index annuities lock in your gains and can't lose value—assuming you play by the rules of the contract and don't surrender early.

Furthermore, these products are considered to be safer than variable types of products because, although FIAs track a market index, the actual value of the annuity's account will not vary from day to day. Rather, it is considered to be much more predictable because the interest credited to the annuity is locked in on a regular basis—typically annually—on the annuity's anniversary date.

Therefore, when the holders of an FIA purchase an annuity, they are still obtaining an insurance contract versus actually purchasing the shares in a stock or equity index.

Because fixed index annuities are, technically, an insurance contract, they can guarantee the safety of investors' principal as well as offer a minimum rate of return. This differs from variable annuity products, which offer the potential for high return yet do not protect the contract holder's principal should the underlying investments perform poorly. In fact, a fixed index annuity can actually guarantee that the value of the account holder's investment will never be less than the sum total of their deposits while still offering the opportunity to exceed the fixed rate of return if growth in the underlying index exceeds the investor's minimum. Overall, a fixed index annuity can provide their holders with both security and stability.

Therefore, a fixed index annuity can be considered as simply a fixed annuity that also offers its holder an optional or extra feature in that it utilizes the underlying index to obtain the amount of interest that will be applied after a certain period of time. When assembled with a lifetime income rider, the fixed index annuity can be a retirement powerhouse for the right individual.

Differences from Other Types of Annuities

A fixed index annuity will differ from other types of annuities primarily in the way that interest is credited to the account value. For example, while a typical fixed annuity will only credit the interest to the underlying account based on a set rate, a fixed index annuity credits interest that is determined by using a formula based on changes in the underlying index it is tracking.

The particular formula used in coming up with a fixed index annuity's return will essentially determine how the additional interest, if any, will be credited. Also, the amount of additional interest the annuity holder receives—as well as when they receive the interest—will depend on the features of the particular fixed index annuity itself.

How Fixed Index Annuities Came About

FIA products have been in existence in the United States for approximately twenty years. Originally created as a mutual fund alternative, these annuities allow their holder to participate in growth linked to the market, yet they prevent the risk of substantial loss of principal that can be associated with other types of equity-related investments. Over time, they have become one of the leading safe-money alternatives to CDs and bonds. When combined with the fact that these indexed annuities can also provide a lifetime income stream (CDs and bonds are unable to produce lifetime income), it is no surprise that sales are taking off with baby boomers. Additionally, because of the loss-protection factor, fixed index annuities have become particularly popular with retirees and pre-retirees concerned with safety of principal and in light of the up and down nature of the stock market.

Technically, a fixed index annuity is a modernization in the design of a regular fixed annuity. For many years, individuals have purchased fixed annuities for the purpose of protecting their savings, planning for retirement, attaining interest growth, and creating retirement income. Regular fixed annuities have, historically, offered a fairly competitive interest rate over time. Yet, similar to many other types of conservative savings options, the rates of interest traditionally offered by regular fixed annuities have been tied to the general level of interest rates in the economy.

In attempting to find a way to generate higher rates of interest on fixed annuities, the fixed index annuity was conceived. Similar to the traditional fixed annuity, this new and improved product offers underlying guarantees while, also, providing the potential for higher returns by having the interest tied to the performance of a stock market index.

Over the years, the cash inflows to fixed index annuities have literally exploded—from roughly $3 billion in 1997 to more than $30 billion by 2009. And during the time of the financial crisis in the United States in 2008 and 2009, growth of FIAs was exponential. In 2011, total FIA sales exceeded $32 billion and many expect 2012 to be much larger. In fact, many of the big name insurance companies like Prudential, Hartford, and Mass Mutual have recently focused primarily on variable annuities. However, all three of them are introducing their first fixed index annuity this year to keep up with the demand for "safe annuities" that baby boomers need.

Industry Annuity Sales
per billions

Year	Variable Annuity	Fixed Annuity	Fixed Indexed Annuity	FIA % of Fixed Annuities
1997	$87.9	$38.2	$2.8	3.9%
1998	$99.5	$32.0	$4.3	9.4%
1999	$121.8	$41.7	$5.1	10.3%
2000	$137.2	$52.7	$5.4	10.2%
2001	$112.8	$71.5	$6.5	9.1%
2002	$119.3	$103.8	$11.7	11.3%
2003	$129.2	$87.6	$14.0	16.0%
2004	$133.5	$90.9	$23.3	26.7%
2005	$137.0	$80.0	$27.2	34.0%
2006	$160.0	$78.0	$25.3	32.4%
2007	$184.0	$73.0	$25.1	34.4%
2008	$156.0	$109.0	$26.7	24.5%
2009	$127.0	$107.9	$30.1	27.9%

Source: Google Images

In some instances, even though FIAs are considered to be more conservative than equity-related investments, the returns that have been gained on fixed index annuities have been higher than the index benchmarks they were credited from. Recall that with "annual reset," we never have to make up any losses on the negative years. So any positive gains will automatically be added on top of our previous gains. This gives FIAs the ability to actually outperform the indexes that they mirror.

Phases of a Fixed Index Annuity

Typically, similar to other types of annuities, fixed index annuities have two different phases. The first is what is referred to as the accumulation phase. This phase begins as soon as the investor starts making deposits into the annuity. During this time, the investor makes deposits into the account—or deposits one lump sum—and these funds begin to earn interest within the account.

One big advantage is that the FIA account holder will receive at least a guaranteed amount of interest credited to the account. This interest is guaranteed by the insurance company or by an interest rate that is based upon the growth of an external index. In addition, the investor will defer having to pay taxes on this interest until they begin receiving their withdrawals—allowing their funds in the account to grow faster.

The accumulation phase can continue for as long as the annuity owner chooses. Many times, annuity owners will execute a non-qualified tax free exchange (known as a "1035 tax free exchange") where the entire accumulation amount is rolled over into a new annuity after the surrender charge is over. In this case, the entire value would move into a new annuity and the entire amount would remain tax deferred. The reason for this would be to take advantage of a higher potential rate, bonus, or new income rider.

The same concept applies to qualified money except it would be referred to as a qualified rollover or transfer into a new annuity.

Finally, in other cases, the accumulation phase is followed by the distribution phase. It is during this time that the investor receives an income stream from their funds in the FIA account. This phase begins at the time that the account holder starts to receive their income payments.

The payments received by the investor may be in the form of a scheduled annuitization (stream of regular income payments) over a certain period of time, including an indefinite time period such as for the remainder of the account holder's life. Furthermore, with the addition of a GLIB (income rider), the annuity owner will have the ability to achieve higher-than-average income growth returns while in deferral that can be used at a later date for lifetime income. We will cover this in more depth shortly.

Many annuities also offer a death benefit option whereby a named individual or individuals may, depending on the situation, receive some or all of the deposited funds that have not yet been returned to the annuity holder, should they pass away.

The Key Players in a Fixed Index Annuity

When considering a fixed index annuity, it is important to understand who all of the entities involved are. There are three primary participants involved in all fixed index annuities. These include the following:

- **Contract holder/investor/annuitant** – In many cases, the contract holder (investor/owner) is also the annuitant, although they do not have to be one in the same. An annuitant is the individual who receives the income benefits from an annuity. The annuity contract holder (owner) is the one responsible for making decisions about the vehicle, such as when withdrawals will begin and who the beneficiary is.

- **Insurance company** – Because annuities are considered to be insurance contracts, they are issued by insurance companies. It is the insurance company that also backs up the annuity's interest and income guarantees.

- **Beneficiary** – FIAs also allow for a beneficiary in the contract. This is the individual (or individuals) who will receive the annuity's death benefit. By naming a beneficiary on the contract, the FIA holder can avoid these funds going into probate should they pass away. Keep in mind that the beneficiary can also be a trust on these annuities.

Investment Return Factors in FIAs

Typically, at the time an investor purchases a fixed index annuity, they can decide which of the indexes (if there is more than one option available) the annuity's value will be allocated to. In addition, the annuity holder is also able to choose which type of crediting method will be utilized in tracking the changes in their chosen index(es). There are different factors involved in tracking these changes.

These factors include:

- **Cap** – Certain types of FIAs set a maximum rate of interest—also referred to as a "cap rate"—the annuity can earn within a certain period of time. Should the fixed index annuity holder choose an index that's increase is more than the cap amount, then the cap rate is used in determining the annuity holder's interest. The specified periods of interest calculation may be either monthly or annually. Think of the cap as a ceiling on how much you can make in a given period.

- **Participation rate** – An FIA's participation rate determines how much of the underlying index's increase will be used in computing the indexed interest rate. For example, if an FIA holder's annuity uses a participation rate of 100 percent, then the annuity would receive 100 percent of the indexed interest achieved within a certain time period.

It is important to note that this calculation also assumes there is not a cap or spread that applies, and that an annuity's participation rates are typically applied after the annuity's cap but before the spread (if applicable). We recommend speaking to a retirement income specialist about caps, participation rates, and spreads.

- **Spread** – With some fixed index annuities, the indexed interest amount will be determined by subtracting a certain percentage from any gain the underlying index achieves within a certain period of time. For instance, should the annuity have a spread of 3 percent and the index increases by 9 percent, the annuity will be credited with 6 percent indexed interest. Keep in mind that the majority of fixed index annuities do not have a spread associated with them.

For those considering the purchase of a fixed index annuity, it is important to understand that there is no one specific method of crediting interest that will consistently deliver the most interest given different market conditions over time. The actuaries at the insurance companies try their best to create options that will all end up with similar returns of the term of your annuity.

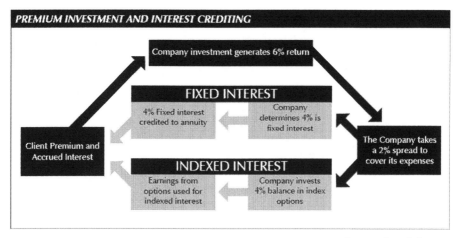

PREMIUM INVESTMENT AND INTEREST CREDITING

Company investment generates 6% return

FIXED INTEREST

4% Fixed interest credited to annuity

Company determines 4% is fixed interest

Client Premium and Accrued Interest

The Company takes a 2% spread to cover its expenses

INDEXED INTEREST

Earnings from options used for indexed interest

Company invests 4% balance in index options

Source: Google Images

Fixed index annuities are different from other types of regular fixed annuities primarily in the way that they credit interest to the account value. While some of the more traditional annuities credit their interest based on a rate set at the time of contract issue, others credit the interest to the annuity contract based on what is referred to as an annual reset.

FIAs, however, credit interest to the account by using a formula based on the changes in the underlying index to which the FIA is linked. It is through these formulas that the additional rate of interest is decided, if any, and then subsequently calculated and credited to the annuity's account. And, to reiterate, the credit can only be flat or positive. A negative credit to a fixed index annuity is not possible based on a standard FIA with no riders attached.

Some of the ways interest is credited to an FIA—taking into account the annuity's cap, spread, and participation rate—include the following:

- **Monthly average** – Using the monthly average method of interest crediting, the individual monthly values of the underlying index (or indexes) are totaled, after which the total is divided by twelve in order to determine the monthly average. So if you had your funds allocated to the S&P 500 index, you would see twelve different S&P 500 numbers (for instance 1100, 1125, 1127, 1101, 1097, etc.) that would be added together and divided by twelve.

In this case, the beginning index value is subtracted from the average in order to determine the amount of either positive or negative index change. This amount is then divided by the beginning value in order to decipher the percentage of interest to be credited to the fixed index annuity.

- **Monthly sum** – Using the monthly sum method of crediting interest, the individual monthly increases and decreases in the index values are tracked and added up. The sum helps in determining the indexed interest to be credited to the FIA. So at the end of the policy anniversary, the company would add up twelve different monthly percentage rates. If the number adds up to be positive, you keep every bit of it. If it is negative, you simply take a zero.

- **Annual point-to-point** – The annual point-to-point method of crediting interest tracks changes in the underlying market index from one contract anniversary of the annuity to the next. It then credits interest based on that annual change. So with annual reset, you are really only concerned with two numbers. The beginning index value on day 1 and the ending index value on day 365.

The chart below shows an example of the fixed index annuity point-to-point interest crediting method in relation to the underlying S&P 500 index.

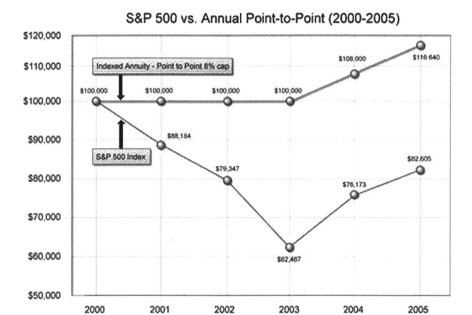

S&P 500 vs. Annual Point-to-Point (2000-2005)

Source: www.ohioinsureplan.com

One popular method of determining the change in the relevant index over the period of the annuity is called the "high-water mark." This method takes a look at the index value at various times during the annuity contract. Traditionally, an annual basis was used, but in this interest-rate environment, most high-water mark products will not let you lock in gains without some caveat to encourage you to stay in the product for the entire duration.

The high-water mark method takes the highest of the values and compares it to the underlying index level at the start of the term. More than likely, using this particular technique may credit more interest than some of the other interest-crediting methods, and it also helps the annuity holder protect against potential market declines. However, when using the high-water mark method, it is important to note that because the interest is not credited to the account until the end of the term, an early surrender may not credit any gain at all to the annuity holder. In addition, any fees, cap rate, and/or participation rate will also affect the amount credited.

Another factor that FIA holders need to be aware of is the automatic annual reset. This factor is typically found in most fixed index annuity contracts. This feature allows the FIA's index values to automatically reset at the end of each contract year. As the previous graphics in this chapter have shown, annual reset is one of the most powerful features of a fixed index annuity. What this means is that the prior year's ending value will become the following year's beginning value in the annuity. In addition, the automatic annual reset feature will lock in any interest that the fixed index annuity has earned during the year. Therefore, in essence, a negative index return from one year will not have an effect on the next year's potential for indexed interest.

As an example, if an annuity is purchased that has an annual reset feature and the underlying market is down, then although no interest is credited to the fixed index annuity account, the annuity holder will also incur no losses and the annuity's value will automatically "reset" on its anniversary date at the same amount it was the prior year. If, however, the underlying market has a positive return in a given year, the fixed index annuity will be credited with the gain and will reset on its anniversary date at the higher amount. This amount will then become the new base amount.

Overall, by including the reset feature in the FIA, the FIA holder will earn no interest in down market years, but they will also never lose any value. Therefore, the annual reset feature provides opportunity for higher return when the underlying index is up and protection when the index is down.

In addition, with annual reset on an FIA, the underlying index will not have to make up for previous losses in order for the annuity's account value to earn additional interest. This is because each contract year, the ending value of the annuity becomes the next year's beginning value.

The graphic below highlights the annual reset feature on a fixed index annuity. It shows the actual S&P 500 historical data between January 1, 2000, and January 1, 2010.

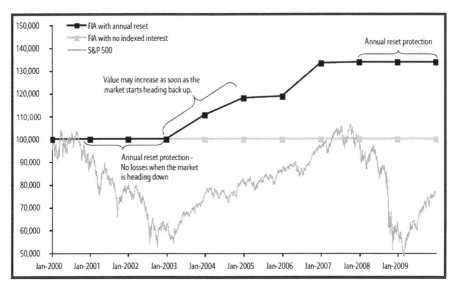

Source: *Fixed Index Annuities: What Are the Advantages of Annual Reset?* (Allianz 2011)

Growing Funds Despite the Roller-Coaster Stock Market

A fixed index annuity can provide the opportunity for potential growth from interest that is based on changes in one or more underlying market indexes. Thus, these products can offer their holders accumulation. And a nice advantage of fixed index annuities versus direct equity-based products is that FIAs do not directly participate in any actual stock or equity investments. In other words, an investor in a fixed index annuity can reap the benefits of growth in a particular index without actually purchasing shares of any stock or index fund. Of course, there is no such thing as a free meal, which means that the downside would be you could be capped out at how much you make in any single year. But in most cases, the cap on the upside far outweighs the floor on the downside (you can't get anything less than a zero).

Some fixed index annuities provide one underlying index to track while others may offer investors a choice of several. In the latter case, FIA holders can choose what portion of their annuity's value will be based on each of the indexes selected. Once the FIA holder begins the accumulation phase of the annuity, the insurance company uses a crediting method to track the performance of the index (or indexes) followed by the annuity. Then, at the end of each contract year, the annual indexed interest is calculated.

Should the result of the annual indexed interest be positive, the investor will automatically receive indexed interest (typically subject to a cap or spread). Another nice advantage of FIAs is that the positive interest gained in the contract is locked in each year, and, unlike other market-related investments, this interest cannot ever be lost—even if the annuity's underlying index declines in the future.

Being a repeater, should the FIA holder's annual interest be negative, essentially nothing happens. Here again, with an FIA, investors cannot lose money due to negative performance of the underlying index—a very different picture than funds invested in an IRA or 401(k) account. This is possible because the holder of an FIA is not directly participating in equities in the index. Therefore, even though the FIA investor does not obtain account growth in negative years, they also do not experience a decline in value of the annuity.

Based on a study by the Wharton Financial Institutions Center, many fixed index annuities have credited an average of anywhere from 4 percent to 8 percent over the past fifteen years. This is in comparison to an average equity fund investment between the years 1990 and 2009 of only 3.17 percent—just a little over one-third of the 8.2 percent S&P 500 return over the same period of time. And the equity investments did not provide the safety and protection of investor principal offered by fixed index annuities. (Keep in mind that with current caps and rates in today's all-time-low interest-rate environment, historical numbers are just that… historical. Do not expect to receive 8 percent returns on today's FIAs, bonds, CDs, or even on Wall Street.)

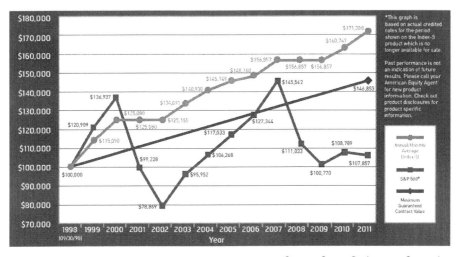

Source: Smart Retirement Strategies

However, today's fixed indexed annuities are not built to make 8 percent average returns. These annuities were built to get a tax-deferred return that is higher than what CDs and bonds are returning at any given period of time. Today, CDs and bonds are at all-time lows due to the interest-rate environment. And based on what the Federal Reserve is saying, these low rates are, most likely, going to stay around for at least a couple of years.

With that is mind, it is easy to understand why the GLIB income riders can be so important today. As I write this, there are income riders that can be attached to FIA's in the range of 7 percent to 10 percent per year. However, these high returns are not attributable to your accumulation and you cannot walk away with them after your surrender charges are over. High annual gains are only beneficial if you decide to turn on a lifetime income stream. You will see from some real-life examples in the following chapter just how powerful income riders can be. In fact, in combination with annual reset, GLIBs are one of the keys to making fixed index annuities a powerful retirement tool.

Growing Funds Despite the Roller-Coaster Stock Market

An old concept that many of the top retirement income specialists use in regards to annuities is the "split concept" or "multi-bucket approach" to income. The split annuity concept would be ideal for a client who needs income immediately (or in the first few years) but doesn't want to have all of his or her money go to an SPIA (single premium immediate annuity - As the name implies, these annuities usually start making regular monthly payments to you *immediately* after you turn over the funds to the insurance company) and wants to make sure that he or she gets the biggest bang for the buck. In a split annuity, the first "bucket" could be a five-year immediate annuity that would generate enough income to meet the client's needs for the next five years. The second bucket would be a fixed index annuity with a lifetime income benefit rider that would grow deferred for five years and then create a lifetime income on day one of year six when the first bucket runs dry. This method is used to maximize your income while retaining the control and maintaining the flexibility you lose by having it all go into an SPIA.

There is also the growing concept that no single annuity can meet any one person's needs. The best income annuities are usually some of the worst accumulation annuities and vice versa. With this in mind, you can see how it can make sense to allocate your funds to multiple types of fixed index annuities to take advantage of the strengths each one brings to the table. For instance, instead of your entire retirement nest egg going into the top income annuity, you could have a part of it go into the income annuity, a piece go into a shorter term accumulation annuity, and even a third piece go into a big bonus annuity with longer duration but very high upside. In that scenario, you have taken advantage of income, short-term growth with the opportunity to upgrade your annuity after the surrender, and long-term growth that can turned into income down the road or used for 10 percent free withdrawals each year.

Taking Advantage of Tax-Deferred Growth

The interest earned within a fixed index annuity is tax-deferred. For those who deposit funds into their fixed index annuity with after-tax dollars, the only tax due upon withdrawal will be calculated from the growth of the account's earnings.

This means that the funds inside of a fixed index annuity will not be taxed until they are withdrawn, giving the holder a nice advantage over other types of direct investment choices such as mutual funds, stocks, and CDs. In many instances, a long-term fixed index annuity may even outperform CDs, bonds, and treasuries. And, although these products were not designed to outperform the popular stock- and equity-related indexes, many fixed index annuities did so during the recent recession when the stock market performed poorly.

While investors can also obtain the advantage of tax-deferred growth in retirement accounts such as 401(k) plans and IRAs, the big difference lies in the fact that annuities do not have any government-imposed contribution limits. This means that annual contribution maximums do not apply, allowing FIA holders to save a great deal more on an annual basis than they are allowed to with most other tax-advantaged types of retirement savings options. It is not uncommon to see high-net-worth Americans put millions of dollars away into these retirement vehicles. Not to mention that the FIA retirement option can't go down in value like its counterpart, the 401(k) plan.

The tax-deferral feature on a fixed index annuity, coupled with the ability to make larger deposits, can help an investor's funds grow exponentially—especially if those funds are invested for the long term. Combined with the power of annual reset, principal protection, and lifetime income riders, we hope you can see why these can be superior retirement vehicles over everything you have been taught up to this point.

Accessing a Guaranteed Retirement Income

Fixed index annuities are not just used to accumulate savings but, also, to provide an income to the holder. With this in mind, those who own a fixed index annuity have the ability to access their funds in a number of different ways.

Many FIA contracts allow interest to be paid out on a monthly, quarterly, semiannual, or annual basis to the recipient from a fixed amount option. In addition, most fixed index annuities also permit the holder to access up to 10 percent of the accumulated account value every year—beginning with the thirteenth month of ownership—without incurring a withdrawal penalty or surrender charge. Any withdrawals in excess of 10 percent of the account's value are subject to a withdrawal penalty. In addition, similar to retirement accounts, withdrawals are also typically subject to income taxation at the recipient's ordinary income tax rate as well as a 10 percent IRS early withdrawal penalty if the FIA holder is under age 59½.

In most fixed index annuities, the surrender charges decline over time on an incremental basis until they eventually disappear. The time frame on fixed index annuity surrender charges can typically range between one to fifteen years, depending on the actual contract. With this in mind, a fixed index annuity is likely not the best place for investors to put emergency funds or any funds that may need to be accessed quickly. Rather, these vehicles are geared toward long-term nest-egg funds—the funds that investors need to always be there, regardless of how long they live.

One way of increasing the amount of liquidity in a fixed index annuity is that in some contracts, the contract owner receives a bonus that is fully credited to their account on the very first day. Some of these bonuses could be as high as 10 percent. The bonus received could be used to offset the withdrawal fee. Bonuses are also used to help alleviate losses from leaving other retirement vehicles or losses incurred due to stock market volatility.

Certainly, one of the best ways to withdraw funds from a fixed index annuity is to receive a lifetime income from the annuity's account. The income features available today on many FIAs have the ability to increase over time, therefore allowing the FIA owner to keep up with inflation. This is especially important as the income received is likely to be set up for the long term. Usually, these income options take the form of annuitizing the contract or using the GLIB, mentioned previously. In some cases, the issuing insurance company will even guarantee increases up to a certain percentage on their lifetime income riders—typically 3 percent—in order to help offset inflation. This feature is extremely powerful, as only annuities can pay out an increasing amount of income on a decreasing asset.

Therefore, with regard to income, fixed index annuities are extremely flexible. Most contracts offer a number of different income riders that can guarantee a certain amount of payments over time based on the determination from an income withdrawal account. And because certain fixed index annuity accounts can increase the amount of the holder's guaranteed lifetime income payment every year there is a positive interest credit to the account value, the amount of the annuitant's income will never decrease. Therefore, FIAs can truly work well in any market condition. But unlike a 401(k) plan, they can contractually ensure a lifetime income stream regardless of how long you live. The income received from an FIA will pay out as long as the recipient—and their spouse, if that option is elected—lives, and it can even continue to pay out should the contract holder outlive the balance of the account. With features like this coupled with all of the flexibility and control you have, I hope it becoming clear why this is referred to as a "'Savior' Retirement plan."

Providing Asset Protection

Another distinct advantage of holding a fixed index annuity is the asset protection they can provide. These financial vehicles allow investors to essentially transfer the risk to the insurance company.

Over the past decade, investors have faced significant volatility in the market. Many of those who owned mutual funds and stock shares have suffered large losses in their portfolios. This alone has prompted a number of investors to take a closer look at the benefits of fixed index annuities.

Fixed index annuities help investors insulate their savings from potential investment risk due to market volatility. When the performance of the underlying market in an FIA is negative, the annuity contract protects the investor's principal as well as their previously credited amounts of interest. In fact, with a fixed index annuity, the worst case scenario for the annuity holder is that a year with a negative market return is simply a zero-interest year for the FIA holder. Most investors would agree that zero-interest in a down market is much more appealing than investment losses.

The graphic below shows fixed index annuities in comparison to many other types of financial vehicles in terms of the potential for possible growth and possible loss. You will notice that fixed index annuities are not poised to make as high returns as stocks and mutual funds. However, you will notice that they aren't subject to loss like stocks and funds are.

Using a baseball analogy to discuss these concepts is useful. In this case, the stocks would be a home-run hitter who strikes out just as much as he hits home runs. Likewise, the FIA would be a player who consistently hits singles and doubles every game. Although we all know that home-run hitters are exciting to watch and the ones who make the highlight reels (similar to a hot per-forming stock), we also know that baseball games are won by consistent performers who always manage to get on base. If you were a professional baseball manager, which type of player would you pick for your team? I know every manager out there today would take a guy who hits singles and doubles all day long over any home-run/strikeout king.

The protection against investment losses is one of the most sig-nificant advantages offered by fixed index annuities. In highlight-ing the power of the asset protection that fixed index annuities offer, Jack Marrion, President of Advantage Compendium Ltd, made the following statement in the July 2009 issue of *Senior Market*

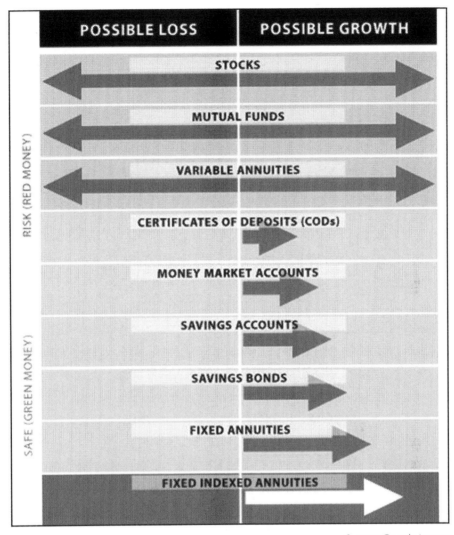

POSSIBLE LOSS	POSSIBLE GROWTH
STOCKS	
MUTUAL FUNDS	
VARIABLE ANNUITIES	
CERTIFICATES OF DEPOSITS (CODs)	
MONEY MARKET ACCOUNTS	
SAVINGS ACCOUNTS	
SAVINGS BONDS	
FIXED ANNUITIES	
FIXED INDEXED ANNUITIES	

RISK (RED MONEY) / SAFE (GREEN MONEY)

Source: Google Images

Advisor: "If you could have purchased an FIA every month, beginning in August 1929, your average annual index annuity return for the Great Depression would have been 6.4%. All of this during a decade that ended 65% lower than when it began."

This degree of asset protection allows FIA holders much more control over their future income, as they will not experience the substantial losses possible when invested directly in the financial markets. In exchange for this protection of assets, FIA holders are typically required to leave their funds deposited in the annuity for a specified amount of time—usually between five and ten years. Should the investor need to withdraw some or all of their funds during this time, they will likely face a surrender penalty from the insurance company. However, should investors treat this as a long-term financial vehicle, the funds in their FIA account, as well as the credited interest, will remain protected.

Providing an Income that Cannot Be Outlived–No Matter How Long

Similar to other types of annuities, a fixed index annuity allows its holder to convert the annuity's value into a series of income payments. With an FIA, these payments can be a fixed amount or they can vary, depending on the contract you buy and/or the income rider. In addition to the income benefits, however, fixed index annuities may also offer additional types of benefits or optional income riders that allow income payments to increase to help keep pace with inflation over time.

FIA holders typically have two choices when it comes to receiving their annuity income, which include annuitization payments or income withdrawals. It is, however, important to note that there are tax differences, depending on which method is chosen.

For example, if an FIA is not held within a qualified retirement account such as an IRA or 401(k) plan—and there are essentially no tax benefits for doing so—a portion of each annuitization payment will be considered a tax-free return of what the annuity holder paid into the annuity and the other portion is considered to be taxable as interest that was earned in the account.

Typically, when the holder of an FIA reaches the age of sixty, the income payments from their FIA can begin at any time. In many cases, should the annuity holder wait until a later date to begin taking their income withdrawals, the amount of their payments will likely increase. It is important to note, though, that the income withdrawals could be subject to the recipient's ordinary income tax rate. And, similar to many other types of retirement accounts, should the FIA holder withdraw funds prior to reaching age 59½, they may incur an IRS penalty of 10 percent for the early withdrawal.

Creating a Comfortable Retirement While Leaving a Legacy for Future Generations

In addition to providing an income that cannot be outlived, fixed index annuities provide another attractive feature in that they can allow their holder to leave a legacy for his or her loved ones. This feature allows the investor to make money available to a named beneficiary or beneficiaries in the event that the investor passes away and did not receive some or all of the income from the annuity contract. Oftentimes, the nominated beneficiary can decide whether they would like to receive the death benefit proceeds in a single lump-sum payment or via a series of regular payments received over time.

Salvaging Current Retirement Plans—It's Never Too Late to Change Course

Regardless of where an individual's funds are now, there are a number of ways to purchase fixed index annuities through either regular or periodic cash deposits or by making one large lump-sum deposit. Today, most people have the ability to roll either a portion of or their entire 401(k) plan into one of these index annuities without having to pay any taxes until a future date when income is accessed. One-time payments are used for funding what is known as "single premium annuities." Conversely, those who prefer to spread their deposits out over time will pursue what is called "periodic funding of the annuity" or "flexible premium annuities."

Single Premium Annuities

With single premium annuities, the purchaser can make their deposit via one lump sum. It is important to note that even though an individual may make their annuity deposit in this manner, the annuity payout period does not need to begin immediately. Rather, the annuity holder may prefer to leave their funds deposited in the annuity to grow over time. Certainly, one of the greatest advantages of a fixed index annuity is the safety of principal, so this might be a good strategy for an investor seeking asset protection over time and an income stream that begins at some later point in the future.

Single premium annuities can also be funded, for example, when an employer's defined benefit pension plan becomes terminated or they leave their job for any reason. Here, the accrued benefits for each of the employee participants may be used to purchase a single premium annuity.

Retirement funding may not always be the ultimate goal of single premium annuities. For instance, an individual may want to fund a single premium annuity if they receive a lump-sum legal settlement. In fact, legal damage awards—and specifically those received in personal injury cases—are often meant to make up for lost future earnings of the plaintiff. Single premium annuities are, therefore, uniquely suited for this, as they can be funded with settlement dollars and then provide regular income payments over the individual's lifetime. Other related single premium annuity funding situations can include cash from settlements received in a divorce or the receipt of an inheritance.

Periodic Annuity Funding

In lieu of funding an annuity with a single lump sum, individuals may choose to fund their annuity on a periodic basis. This means that the annuity will be funded with deposits made over time. There are essentially two ways to fund an annuity on a periodic basis: with a level, or fixed, premium or with a flexible premium.

Level/Fixed Premium Annuities

The method of using level or fixed premiums to fund an annuity entails funding the annuity account with payments made on a regular and ongoing basis. For example, using this method, the annuity holder would have a particular frequency of payments, such as monthly or annually, that is specifically spelled out in the annuity contract.

With level premiums, most issuing insurance companies will require annuity purchasers to pay a regular, agreed-upon fixed amount of deposit. In this case, the annuity holder is not allowed to make a higher or a lower premium amount than is stated in the contract. This type of contract is rare among fixed index annuities.

Fixed level premiums can be compared to a type of forced savings whereby the annuity holder is required to put a set amount of funds into an annuity so that they are assured of having retirement income in later years.

Flexible Premium Annuities

When using a flexible premium deposit approach, the annuity holder will be allowed to make premium deposits at will, meaning that they can make payments into the annuity account at various and irregular times. In flexible premium annuities, the flexibility of adding funds is completely at the discretion of the annuity owner.

In many cases, the issuing insurance company will still send a premium notice to the annuity holder based on a certain frequency—annually, semiannually, quarterly, or monthly—but the individual may decide to pay a different amount than what they are billed for, or they may skip that premium payment altogether. It is important to note, however, that although the flexible premium deposit method does provide a great deal of leeway for the annuity holder in terms of making their deposits, the issuing insurance company is likely to impose at least some amount of minimum and maximum payments to be made.

Free Look Period

All annuity buyers should be aware of the "free look" period that occurs following their annuity purchase. This period of time is considered the "window" that gives the annuity purchaser time to review their annuity contract and to fully contemplate their decision about their purchase. Should, during the free look period, the individual decide they no longer wish to keep their annuity, they will be entitled to a full refund of their premium payments—provided that they officially cancel the contract within this time frame.

The length of the annuity's free look period is actually mandated by each state's Department of Insurance, and these periods may vary from one insurance company to another. Typically, however, most annuities have a free look period of ten days. This period may extend to thirty days, depending on the specific insurance company and the rules of the particular state.

The Bottom Line

Along with the many positive benefits offered with fixed index annuities, there are several considerations that should be taken into account by those thinking about purchasing such an investment vehicle. Every investor's goals are different, so it is imperative that prior to moving forward with the purchase of a fixed index annuity, individuals consider whether or not the following issues are important to them:

- Accumulation of funds based on index-related growth, allowing for the potential of higher returns than a regular fixed annuity

- Deferral of taxes

- Principal protection and the ability to lock in gains every year

- Protection of both retirement assets and income

- Liquidity with regard to flexible withdrawal options

- The ability to make an unlimited amount of contributions

- Preservation of wealth

- Guaranteed income payments

- Flexibility of premium payments

- Leaving a legacy for loved ones, with an option to pass funds directly to heirs and bypass probate

- Peace of mind having a lifetime pension income

If any or all of these apply to you, we highly encourage you to seek out a retirement income specialist as soon as possible.

Fixed Index Annuity Advantages

Fixed index annuities have the distinct advantage of allowing market gains that are attained via a rising market but without the negative return and risk to principal that are due to market losses. Technically, then, an FIA is always moving forward by locking in its prior year's gains. However, an eclipsing advantage from a baby boomer retirement perspective is the ability to create and control a contractually guaranteed lifetime income stream.

For those who find that owning a fixed index annuity to be a good fit, these vehicles can provide a number of financial benefits, including:

- **Lower risk** – An FIA can offer a very effective method for retirement income planning—especially as compared to the stock market. Investments in stocks and other growth-related equity investments may offer the potential for unlimited returns, however, the same investments—as we have all learned over the past decade—can put investors at a much higher degree of risk. Because fixed index annuity holders are not directly investing in stocks or other equities, the underlying risk is essentially eliminated.

- **Higher interest** – Fixed index annuities can also provide a much higher amount of interest than more "conservative" alternatives such as CDs or bonds, while still keeping assets safe.

- **Protection of funds** – Holders of fixed index annuities will never lose the initial amount of principal funds they deposited into the account—and in many cases, even the gains over set periods of time are locked in, resetting the annuity to a new and higher base value. Finally, all fixed index annuities come equipped with minimum guarantees that provide at least a minimum growth rate if you hold the annuity to maturity.

- **Death benefit protection** – For those who wish to ensure that loved ones are taken care of, most fixed index annuities offer a death benefit feature whereby funds in the annuity account that have not been returned to the annuitant may be provided via these proceeds.

Considerations When Choosing a Fixed Index Annuity

Although fixed index annuities may offer a great deal of advantages, not all products are created equal. Therefore, there are a variety of factors that should be considered when choosing to invest in an FIA. First, the overall concept of fixed index annuities can be somewhat confusing. Because of this, it is important to understand all the fine print prior to purchasing such a vehicle.

Primary concerns to be aware of include:

- **Credit rates** – The credit rates associated with fixed index annuities can be especially confusing to some purchasers. These rates refer to the different ways the underlying market index will be tracked in terms of crediting interest to the FIA account. Most of them were explained in this chapter. Some of the more common methods of determining credit rates include the point-to-point monthly method, the monthly average method, and the point-to-point annual method. It is important to understand and thoroughly compare these because, depending on the method chosen, there could be a big difference in the overall return to the fixed index annuity account.

- **Participation rates** – This factor refers to the amount of participation the issuing insurance company is willing to give the annuity holder in the underlying market index being tracked. An example is if the annuity contract allows for a participation rate of 70 percent, the fixed index annuity holder will be allowed to capture 70 percent of the movement of the index. Thus, should the underlying market index have a 10 percent gain in a given year, the annuity holder would be able to take part in 70 percent of that 10 percent gain, or 7 percent. (10 percent market gain × 70 percent participation rate = 7 percent gain to FIA holder.)

- **Caps** – The cap rate on a fixed index annuity determines the maximum amount of interest the insurance company will pay out. This means that the holder of the annuity will only receive a certain maximum amount of interest on the contract.

- **Vesting schedule/surrender penalties** – In most cases, a fixed index annuity will allow the contract holder to withdraw up to 10 percent of the principal balance without incurring a surrender charge. However, it is still important to verify this fact, as well as to determine whether or not there will be any other types of penalties and/or fees.

- **Administrative fees and other related charges** – Most fixed index annuities will *not* have various fees that go toward administrative costs, brokerage costs, overhead, and marketing. These are normally built into the rates the company is offering. Although this is unusual compared to other types of financial instruments, it is a good idea to be aware of the meaning and the amount of potential charges in the rare case they do exist.

- **Income rider fees and types** – Although income riders make a FIA an even more attractive investment vehicle, they always come with a price. And while the charges only come off of the accumulation value (you are not charged for the rider on your income portion), these can be a costly mistake if you are not certain you are going to take advantage of the income. Moreover, there are a few FIA income riders that do not credit your income account with the annual "roll-up" if you take a free withdrawal or required minimum distribution for the year. It is important to speak with a retirement income specialist that truly understands the ins and outs of each income rider.

Some of the other items to be aware of when considering and comparing fixed index annuities include:

- High-interest crediting to allow for growth

- Short surrender period

- Living benefit riders/benefits for needs such as long-term care

- Income riders that can allow lifetime income as well as the ability to pass remaining annuity funds to heirs

- Higher deferred growth of the annuity's income base

- Various indexing options that may be chosen by the annuity holder

Certainly, as with any other financial decision, careful consideration must be taken to ensure that a fixed index annuity holder purchases not just the right product but, also, from the right issuing company. Because the guarantees stated in a fixed index annuity are important, it is essential to consider which company is backing those guarantees—because, ultimately, it is the underlying issuing insurance company that will have the responsibility of backing them.

Therefore, the financial strength and stability of the issuing insurance company must be determined prior to moving forward with the purchase of an FIA. A few ways to ensure the company is strong is to determine the following:

- **Ratings** – Insurance companies are rated, typically using the letters A through F, based on their claims-paying ability and overall financial strength. It is important to stick with the companies that rank higher in these ratings.

- **Management of risk** – Insurance companies are in the business of managing risk. It is, therefore, essential to purchase from a company that has a long track record of successfully hedging against potentially extreme market events.

- **Claims paying ability** – Insurance companies are also in the business of paying claims when their policyholders need them, so going with a company that has a good reputation for doing so is imperative—especially as it relates to the payment of retirement income. Many of these companies have been around for more than one hundred years and have, consequently, weathered some really tough times, including periods like the Great Depression. Although a newer company isn't always a bad thing, there is something to be said for a company that has stood by its promises for multiple generations.

Moving Forward

The bottom line is that those who own fixed index annuities have the ability to participate in a portion of market gains but without the need to take on the risk of loss. This can be an extremely attractive feature—especially for those who have suffered significant investment losses in the past. Even more important are the attractive income riders that can be added on to almost any fixed index annuity to create a lifetime income stream. With annual "roll-up" rates of 7 percent and higher on certain income riders, it is no surprise that these investment vehicles are getting a second look even from skeptics. As the number of baby boomers entering retirement and looking for sources of lifetime income rises, these fixed index annuities will continue to be among the top retirement solutions.

FIAs allow their holders to be involved with the underlying market and to benefit from upward performance while being protected from any type of significant or unexpected market losses. Those who tend to be good candidates for these products include investors who wish for a secure income in retirement without the need to micromanage a portfolio or worry about the potential for a market loss at any given time. Fixed index annuities also help protect their holders from excessive taxation as well as assuage fears of outliving retirement income, and are often favored over alternative investments such as treasuries, bonds, and CDs that typically offer safety but, also, lower returns.

Once an investor is ready to withdraw their funds, they can create a retirement income scheme that works best for their specific scenario—one that may provide them with income for the remainder of their life—regardless of how long they live. Their very own safe money private pension plan.

The individuals who take advantage of the flexibility and security offered by fixed index annuities will find themselves in a great position for receiving a lifetime of market-linked income that can increase over time and will never decrease due to market downturns. It is this combination of downside protection and upside interest earnings potential that is truly the key of a fixed index annuity's security and appeal. Because of these factors, fixed index annuity financial vehicles can truly be considered the best of all worlds for both accumulating retirement savings and ensuring long-term retirement income.

Phase 6: The Safe Money Retirement Plan For You

By James Cline

"The Doctor in Search of a Retirement Diagnosis"

I met a client on the golf course a few years back. Anytime the day gets a little stressful, I shoot over to the golf course to unwind. Usually, I play a round by myself, but this particular day, I was paired up with a physician. Come to find out, I'm not the only one that likes to swing and hit things when stress is involved. I usually concentrate on my game and avoid talking a lot, but that day, I wanted to vent and air out all the crummy things that had happened in my world that day. After groveling about my horrible day, my new doctor friend, John, began telling me about his retirement concerns. As it turns out, my little computer virus was nothing compared to what the doctor was stressing about.

One of his colleagues had been doing all the right things his whole life as far as savings, but he didn't have the proper planning to make his money work for him in the best way possible.

Sure, his colleague had a nice savings account, mutual funds, and other retirement accounts, but his IRA—which had grown to nearly $500,000, even after a 10 percent decrease one month before—was his biggest concern. He needed it to produce $30,000 per year for him, but it was nowhere close to being guaranteed for life. To make matters worse, it was also going to be fully taxable. What the doctor thought was $500,000 was really closer to $375,000 after taxes. And that was assuming the tax rates didn't go up.

Now, granted, John's retirement date was still a few years out, but he was in the same boat as his colleague. His concerns were increasing tax rates, market volatility, and wealth transfer. The doctors concerns were valid. But what solution could I offer to help provide him with the guarantees he needed now and, also, help him deal with his later tax liability? Believe it or not, I was able to tell him everything was going to be OK, which made his next shot into the woods a little bit easier to swallow. I told him I couldn't help him with his slice, but I could help him lower his tax liability on the $500,000 of IRA money, which was going to be fully taxable. I also let him in on the private pension annuity secret where an insurance company can contractually guarantee exactly what his income would be at retirement. Finally, I revealed the annual reset secret of the fixed index annuity that would certify that his money would never go down due to market fluctuations. He couldn't believe it. That had to have been the best round he ever played—even though half his shots went into the woods. He didn't have a care in the world because I showed him how a fixed index annuity was going to relieve all his stresses.

John had also done quite well when it came to saving and investing. Of course, now he was on the back nine of his career and wanted to get into the clubhouse without losing any strokes. John had just turned sixty and, under his current plan, expected to fully retire at age sixty-five. In John's case, one of the main advantages is that he still had some time to plan and get himself on the right course for retirement.

The plan we devised for John was clean and simple: convert his retirement money to a Roth IRA, place the Roth IRA into a fixed index annuity, retire in five years, and receive income tax free on that amount forever. What is even better is that whatever amount is left over goes to the beneficiaries' tax free. We took John's current traditional IRA out of risky mutual funds and transferred it to a safe-money alternative: the fixed index annuity. We withheld some of John's money to help pay taxes at the end of the year, but we used a bonus to get his fund back to the total original amount. We also attached an income rider that would grow the income account by a stated percentage. All this meant that John's investment would be able to produce more than $30,000 of tax-free income per year, for life in five years from now. Now, *that's* what I call a hole in one.

Before you embark on any type of financial retirement planning, always consult a retirement income specialist you know and trust—one that always has your best interest in mind. All too often, I see clients in frustrating situations where we are left cleaning up a mess left by their previous financial advisor.

"The Engineer's Family"

Fixed index annuities are not only used by people gearing up for guaranteed retirement income. In fact, they can be a good fit for a wide range of needs and people. I sat in on an appointment with an advisor and good friend of mine a few weeks back. He met a couple, Cliff and Connie, at one of his educational workshops that he gives a couple of times a month. Cliff was a retired engineer and was worried about what he was going to leave behind to his wife and daughter. Yes, income was a need, but Cliff's health was also starting to fade, and he was worried about high nursing home costs, which, at the time, were $70,000 a year. Cliff also wanted to know how he could maximize his estate to leave as much as he could to his family. Life insurance and long-term care (LTC) weren't feasible for Cliff because of his health issues, but we did have other options for him.

All fixed index annuities are a little different, but some offer benefits that assist with LTC and wealth transfer. Cliff was out of options for traditional LTC insurance and life insurance, but an FIA was a perfect option for him. Cliff had already been turned down by most companies despite the fact that, like most of us, he had worked and saved his entire life to leave as much as he could to his wife and daughter. The fixed index annuity that Cliff chose encompassed all the options he needed and wanted in one product. Some of the benefits Cliff's particular FIA had included an increase of 6.5 percent per year that could be left to his beneficiaries but that could also serve as income that could double if he were unable to perform two out of six daily-living activities. Some clients believe they should self-insure, but why would you ever use your own money when you can use someone else's?

Of course when this product was presented to Cliff, he couldn't believe that he could withdraw funds for income—funds that could double if he became disabled—and also be guaranteed funds to be left to his family. It was a win-win-win for Cliff. It was like a "buy-one-get-two-free" sale.

But we weren't done yet. Remember Karen, Cliff's wife? She was in her mid-fifties and wanted to know what we could suggest for her retirement planning. Karen was upset because she had worked hard her entire life but was losing money. Karen was ahead of the game but was tired of putting money away month after month only to see her retirement fund go down. Income was not as a big a concern for Karen as her it was for her father. Accumulation and keeping her money safe were Karen's two biggest concerns. It was a good thing we were all sitting down because Karen couldn't believe the features offered by FIAs.

Most FIAs offer the greatest financial instrument feature ever invented: annual reset. Annual reset does exactly what it sounds like it does—it resets the beginning index value every year, regardless of what happened in the stock market the previous year. Not only do your gains lock in but you also lock in your spot in the market every year. Let me give you an example. Let's say you invest $100,000 into an FIA and the S&P 500 is at 1,000 points. In the first year, the market goes down 20 percent. With your money invested in an FIA, you wouldn't lose a dime—your $100,000 would still be there—but your new starting point in the S&P 500 would be at the lower amount (800 points). Now, when the market drops 20 percent, it will often rebound the next year (at least that is what your broker will probably tell you, right?). So let's say that the market does correct itself the next year and still doesn't get back to where we started at 1,000 points. We are close, but only at 960 points. In Karen's case, she would calculate the return on her original $100,000 even though the S&P 500 still hasn't made it back to where it started. Karen couldn't believe it. What better way, in a volatile market, to lock in your gains every year? Karen nailed it when she said, "It's like an elevator with no down button. In the down years, we stay flat, and in the positive years, we move up." Karen was exactly right.

"The Small Business Owner"

Small business owners have limited options when it comes to investing for retirement. When you consider how volatile the economy has been the past few years, it is no wonder so many small businesses are barely hanging on. Small business owners already have a tremendous amount of stress from the day-to-day operations of running a business, but retirement planning can be one of the biggest stresses of all. With all the limitations and contribution limits enforced with traditional IRAs, Roth IRAs, and 401(k) plans, contributing to a SEP (Simplified Employee Pension) IRA can be one of the best opportunities for small business owners.

Where, exactly, can we put our hard-earned money earmarked for retirement? Sure, there are CDs, bonds, mutual funds, and stocks, but none of these can necessarily provide the lifetime guarantees needed when planning for retirement. We all want the upside of what the market can potentially provide without the downside. We know that CDs can provide needed guarantees, but who wants to make only 1 percent on their money today? Wouldn't it be great if we could have the best of both worlds? Believe it or not, we can. There exists a product capable of increasing our retirement account funds almost three times more than what any other investment vehicle can. What is it you ask? Keep reading to find out.

First of all, business owners receive tax deductions for any contributions made to a SEP IRA, but they also have the flexibility of deciding each year how much they would like to contribute. It would nice if every year were a growth year, but in reality, some years aren't as good as others. How much the IRS allows one to contribute to a SEP IRA changes over time, but as inflation increases, so do contribution limits. I will discuss our options for keeping up with inflation later.

What if someone told you that if you put a certain amount of money away for a certain number of years, they could tell you exactly what your income would be for the rest of your life? I will tell you the rest of the story later...

As a small business owner myself, I am certainly familiar with the expenses and debt in the early years of starting a business. Because of this, setting money aside for savings is usually not at the top of a new business owner's list of financial priorities. But the IRS allows small business owners to contribute more money to a SEP IRA than any other retirement plan out there. Moreover, a SEP IRA allows small business owners to catch up for lost time. Once a business has been established and achieves success, cash flow generally increases—and that is precisely the best time to invest as much as possible. And keep in mind, it's tax deductible.

Now that we have decided what type of contribution we want to make, we have to make sure we invest our money in something that will be there when we need it. The ideal choice would be an investment vehicle that contractually guarantees our retirement nest egg will provide enough income for us throughout our later years. An FIA with an income rider as the investing vehicle housing our SEP IRA contributions is one of the best ways to ensure our money will be there when we need it.

There are multiple reasons an FIA is such an attractive option for these monies. Number one: the investment product will match each contribution up to a certain percentage, usually every year you contribute. Likewise, using an FIA with a bonus that allows continued contributions while still giving a bonus to future contributions can be a great way to catch up for lost time. Number two: we could also attach an income rider that increases the income account by another stated percentage increase. Every year, not only will you receive the initial bonus the product gives on any contributions but you will receive another credit increase for all monies in the account. Let's look at an actual example of how this might work for someone using products available today. The IRS allows us to contribute 25 percent of our compensation or up to $49,000 a year, whichever is greater. It doesn't have to be the same every year, but for this example, we will use the maximum amount allowed by the IRS.

So, "Small Business Owner Jones," age fifty-eight, contributes $49,000 a year to a SEP IRA for the next seven years with a 10 percent bonus, and we attached an income rider that will credit the account at 7 percent. That is a 17.7 percent compound per year on every contribution Small Business Owner Jones makes for the next few years. The compounded interest on Small Business Owner Jones's funds adds up to $499,101 in seven years. Pretty amazing, isn't it? Remember that this is a *retirement* account, and Small Business Owner Jones is building this for an income in his retirement years. Small Business Owner Jones still has the flexibility of cashing out the account if he needs to, but he wants to be able to take the income out over time. This is Small Business Owner Jones's private pension, which can be viewed as his own personal 401(k) matching plan. It matches and guarantees more than any other 401(k) plan or pension plan available today. Small Business Owner Jones now has a retirement nest egg that he can turn into income for the rest of his life.

So what would this look like? Small Business Owner Jones has all this money in his guaranteed income account, so what kind of income can he get? Using the guarantees available today, he can take 4.75 percent of $499,101, which works out to be $23,707 for the rest of his life. And Small Business Owner Jones has the flexibility to start or stop this income at any time—even if his account value ever dropped to zero, *he would still receive this income for the remainder of his life.* It is absolutely amazing that he could contribute to a SEP IRA for only seven years before retirement, still receive a tax deduction, and be guaranteed that much income for the rest of his life.

This information can be one of the most powerful tools available when planning for retirement. That is what building your own safe money private pension is about. People save their entire lives and, yet, there is nothing else on Earth that can guarantee income like this for the rest of their lives—especially years down the road when they need it the most.

"The Retiring Corporate Manager"

I was on a plane flying to Atlanta when I had the pleasure of meeting a corporate manager for a logistics company named Scott. He had just turned sixty-five and was ready to retire immediately. Scott's two main concerns were income now and income later—income he hoped would continue to rise (even in retirement) and keep up with inflation. He made a great a point when he said, "My whole life I was able to earn a raise in salary, why would I want to stop earning a raise in retirement?" Scott's goal required a little more strategic planning, but that's when I introduced him to the concept of bucket annuity planning.

The main concept of bucket annuity planning is to position your assets in different accounts, or "buckets," and have them pour money back out during different time frames. Immediate income is a necessity, but cost-of-living increases are not something to overlook—think back to how much gas cost just ten years ago. So far, in the examples we have looked at, everyone was planning for their future income needs, but in the case of the Scott, we needed to plan for now as well.

Money needed today has to be invested in a different manner from money needed in the future. I told Scott that he should use money he had invested in CDs that were earning less than 1 percent and place those funds into a single premium immediate annuity, also known as an SPIA. This would be the first bucket that would guarantee him income for the next five years, and he could start it immediately. Basically, it's like giving someone a chunk of money that they invest and the insurance company guarantees they will send you a check every month for a certain time frame. As a bonus, it will come out part interest and part principal. It's like having to pay taxes on only 20 percent of your income. This was definitely going to help decrease his tax liability.

The other bucket he set up would work to replenish what he spent down in previous years. The account was set up to start delivering income in five years and would guarantee him an income for the rest of his life. The income that would start at age 70½ would also satisfy any minimum distributions required by the IRS. I should note, in case you aren't aware, that the government requires you to start taking money out of your qualified retirement accounts at age 70½. They believe that because you haven't touched the money by that age and because it's never been taxed, they want you to start withdrawing it regardless of whether or not you want to do so. It is usually only around 3 percent to 4 percent of whatever IRA monies you have, but the government wants to make sure they receive the taxes on that money.

The investment vehicle we would use that could guarantee Scott the income he needs *and* keep up with inflation is a fixed index annuity with an income rider. Not only would an FIA increase his income value a certain percentage to provide him with the level of income he requires, it would also increase every year in which the market made positive gains. I feel this is one of the strongest features of the product. His income would never decrease, and when his plan's funds increased based on market performance, they would stay at that level until the next market increase. Based on hypothetical scenarios at the time, it was estimated that his income would almost double within twelve years. How's that for a raise?

For this particular situation, only two buckets were needed. But I have seen scenarios involving three, four, or even five buckets from which to draw income. It just depends on your situation and income needs.

Phase 7: The Truth About AIG

By Franco Devivo

We all know what happened in 2008: one of the largest financial crashes in US history occurred and shook us to our core. One of the main companies that made headlines during this financial catastrophe was AIG, or American International Group. It took a $182.5 billion bailout by the federal government to keep the company from going bankrupt. As financial planners specializing in annuities, a common question we hear now is, "What if the government had not bailed out AIG? Would every annuity and insurance customer have lost everything?"

This chapter is dedicated to the misconceptions surrounding the AIG fiasco and aims to show you that it was not nearly as scary as you thought. In fact, owners of AIG annuities and life insurance policies were not really in danger of losing anything. This chapter should open your eyes to the strength of insurance companies and why one the perceived safest places to keep your funds (i.e., the bank) is not really as safe as you thought.

Let's start with a bit of history, shall we? AIG was founded in 1919 in China by Cornelius Starr, who moved the company to New York City in 1949. The main focus of the company was personal insurance until 1962, when Maurice Greenberg took over management and changed the company's direction to high-margin corporate coverage and investments. In essence, Greenberg started transforming AIG from a personal insurance company into a multiservice financial company with branches in investment banking, derivatives, brokerage, and lending. Although still currently in the insurance business, it was the investment side of the company that was mainly responsible for its collapse. Moreover, the insurance and annuity division of AIG remained one of the only profitable branches of the company throughout the crisis.

In the beginning of 2008, AIG's credit rating was downgraded from "AAA" to "AA," due largely to the financial losses suffered in conjunction with a falling stock price. What does this mean? Well, AIG's noninsurance side of the business (the "investment banking" side) was, basically betting on real estate transactions and buying CDS's, or credit default swaps. CDS's are, in layman's terms, insurance that covers a default (when a company declares bankruptcy and can no longer pay on their promises). The company's original AAA rating allowed them to swap these without collateral. Once they were downgraded, they were forced to carry more collateral in order to continue leveraging their assets. With the housing market beginning its downturn, this led to an immediate cash problem. In fact, this cash problem spiraled out of control and threatened to crash the entire financial structure of the United States. Please notice that through all of this, not once have I mentioned the life and annuity side of the business threatened or playing a part. That is because they are separate entities, and insurance has a few layers of protection in case of a financial disaster.

Let's talk about that protection. There are quite a few things that have to happen for your retirement plan to completely disappear with an insurance company. In effect, there are multiple layers of protection (protection meaning a way to insure and back up the safety and security of your investment dollars) to make it almost impossible for that happen. In the case of AIG, the insurance they sell is largely held by subsidiaries in individual states. That lends retirees the protection of state regulations, which require insurance companies to have reserve funds set aside to avoid financial catastrophe. So in reality, the AIG that received all the negative media attention—and the huge bailout—and the AIG that issues annuities and life insurance are, to a degree, separate companies. There were numerous articles back in 2009 that revealed that it was entirely possible for AIG to go bankrupt and for your insurance policy to still remain intact. Each state requires every insurance subsidy that does business in that state to have enough liquid assets to cover the insurer's current and future obligations and then some. The states do not care who the parent company is or how many other branches they have. They view them as separate companies in each state.

Let's go through an extreme example to help you understand the sequence of events that would take place in order to protect you. Let's say a local insurance company goes into financial strife and declares bankruptcy. One scenario that could happen is that the state insurance commissioner would essentially take over the company. In this scenario, the law states that policyholders would get back 100 cents on the dollar before the company's creditors can collect a single penny.

Another layer of protection is the state guarantee funds. These are pools of money set aside to pay policyholders in the event of complete failure. Every state has different numbers, but generally, it equates to a guarantee of $100,000 in cash option or up to

$300,000 for a benefit for annuity contracts. The guarantee differs from state to state. The benefit could be either a death benefit or a retirement income benefit purchased for a fee. This is where the argument that your money is safer in banks with the FDIC-backed guarantee up to $250,000 comes from. But let's take a closer look at the banking side.

The first bank failure in history was in 1809 (fdic.gov). Many more banks would fail in the next hundred years after that initial failure. This led to the creation of federal deposit insurance (due largely as a result of the Great Depression). From 1930 through 1933, nearly nine thousand banks failed—four thousand of those failed in 1933 alone. President Franklin D. Roosevelt called for a national banking holiday on March 6, the day after his inauguration, and closed all the banks in the country so they could be reevaluated prior to opening. This was the start of the *Emergency Banking Relief Act*—passed only days before the banks reopened—which eventually led to the creation of the Federal Deposit Insurance Corporation, or FDIC. Notice that the "I" in FDIC means Insurance. What most people in America consider the safety net for all of their bank deposits, is none other than a Federal "Insurance" Company. Perhaps now you are starting to understand why we believe Insurance Carriers are the safest place to have your money. In January 1934, the FDIC began insuring deposits. In 2005, the FDIC was made stronger by a law that merged two deposit insurance funds and increased coverage of certain retirement accounts up to $250,000. Notice the word "certain" here.

Checking, savings, CDs, and money market deposit accounts are all protected by the FDIC. Of course, the need for a higher rate of return is paramount in today's financial and retirement strategies. I don't know anyone who is going to retire based solely on the return of their savings account or CD these days. Mutual funds offered by banking institutions are not insured by the FDIC. Mutual funds are investment vehicles made up of pools of money for the purpose of investing in securities such as stocks, bonds, money market instruments, and similar assets (www.investopedia.com). They are operated by money managers who invest the funds' capital in an attempt to produce capital gains and income for investors.

From an investment point of view, anything you own is not insured, even if it is offered through a subsidiary of your bank. The rule of thumb is that if you deposit it and the rates of return are determined by what a bank offers you, it's insured. But that's it.

As big as AIG's failures were on the investment side, we hope you now understand how secure the insurance division of AIG was through all the financial mess. In truth, it actually demonstrates just how safe your money is being held with an insurance company. Because of the tight regulation of insurance carriers and the mandatory separation of entities, many levels of security exist to protect you. So the next time you hear someone claim that you would be crazy to purchase an annuity or life insurance policy because the company "could be" the next AIG, throw them for a loop and say, "I certainly hope so."

Phase 8: The Conclusion

We hope by now that you have a pretty good grasp on what a Safe Money "Savior" Retirement plan is and how it can play a crucial role in fulfilling your retirement dreams. If you walk away with anything from this book, we hope that it would be the realization that *your ultimate retirement goal should be contractual lifetime income.* This can't be achieved through your savings or checking account, it can't be achieved via your 401(k) plan, and it certainly can't be achieved by any stock or mutual fund that Wall Street tries to sell you on. Your only option for contractual lifetime income is either an old-fashioned pension or the twenty-first century pension: the private pension annuity.

This book also didn't serve its purpose unless it opened your eyes to the 401(k) investment swindle we have all been duped by. If the brightest pension portfolio managers in the country had their hands full making sure the retirement funds they managed on a daily basis would provide enough lifetime income for retirees, how in the world is the average American going to do it? In chapter 2, Nathan described that, as a conservative estimate, he will need to amass more than $2.5 million in his 401(k) plan to generate the same lifetime income his parents receive from their teachers pensions. And he didn't even assume that he would be paying taxes on it when he took it out! Is there anyone reading this that doesn't think all tax rates will be going up to pay for the out-of-control spending of our government over the past decade? I think Nathan's retirement number might need to be closer to $4 million for both he and his wife to retire comfortably. How many of your friends do you know that have $4 million in their retirement plan? Based on what we see from clients, not that many. The baby boomer generation, as a whole, is not even remotely prepared for what lies ahead in their retirement.

If you are a baby boomer, think back for a moment on your parent's retirement. Do you recall them being stressed out, on the verge of bankruptcy, and full of fear that they would outlive their money? The vast majority of you should be saying, "No." With any group of people, there are always some exceptions to the rule, but, by and large, the parents of baby boomers had a solid retirement. It was their group that paved the way for what is known as the "Retirement Dream." It was the same group responsible for launching campaigns, commercials, brochures, and even businesses based around the notion that retiring means living out your dreams on the beach, on a sailboat, on the golf course, or relaxing with fellow retirees. Arizona and Florida were huge beneficiaries of all these retirees looking to live the second half of their lives in the sun.

Some critics would say the "Greatest Generation" saved well because they saw firsthand the effects of the Great Depression. They watched their own parents struggle to make ends meet during that horrible time in history. And I won't disagree with that. However, based on that thinking, the baby boomers should have learned firsthand from their parents how to save. But that clearly didn't happen. It keeps bringing us back to the one constant so many in the previous generation benefited from: lifetime pensions.

What else could have caused this wild shift in retirement thinking? Research study after research study reveals that the number one fear of baby boomers is outliving their income. In fact, a study by Allianz, titled *Reclaiming the Future*[4], exposed that more than 90 percent of baby boomers feel there is a huge retirement crisis and have a limited grasp on how much money they will need to retire. But what would really shock baby boomers' parents is that "61 percent of boomers fear outliving their money in retirement more than [they fear] death." No one ever mentioned that in the retirement brochures or commercials of the past!

Why the Ultimate Goal Is Contractual Lifetime Income

We all know the damage the 2008 financial crisis caused to businesses both large and small. It capsized huge companies like Lehman Brothers and Bear Stearns, and it took out many mom-and-pop stores across the country. More than four hundred banks have shut down or been forced to liquidate or sell out since the 2008 financial crisis. You can check out the entire FDIC "Failed Bank List" since the 2008 crisis at www.fdic.gov/bank/individual/failed/banklist.html. For those of you who enjoy finding things on the web, do some simple Internet searches on failed banks; then, do the same with insurance companies. In a world where nearly all information is readily available if you know where to search, you can find just about anything. However, you will notice that you can hardly find any news on insurance companies failing during this same time period. There are no websites dedicated to listing the "Failed Insurance Companies." There are no blogs from consumers voicing their animosity about losing their annuity or

[4] https://www.allianzlife.com/retirement/research/reclaiming_the_future/reclaiming_the_future.aspx

life insurance premium. And you don't see any sites that discuss the steps you need to take in order to apply for your annuity or life insurance money back like that of a bank deposit at a failed bank. Why? Because these insurance companies are some of the most secure and solid American business structures our country has even seen. And to put it simply, they didn't over leverage and they didn't fail!

Many of these insurance giants have weathered the best of times and the worst of times for hundreds of years. From the Great Depression to the savings and loan crisis in the 1980s and '90s to the 2000 tech crash to the 2008 financial collapse, insurance companies remained resilient. There are more than 2,500 life insurance, property and casualty, and health insurance companies in the United States today. These companies collectively own, manage, and control trillions of dollars; are legally restricted from maliciously leveraging their assets the way banks can; and have reserve funds for financial emergencies, on top of the assets under management.

So many times we hear consumers and financial professionals discuss the importance of only dealing with "A"-rated insurance carriers. And we couldn't agree more—the ratings are very important. What we find interesting, however, is the number of Americans that have no issues with putting their entire life savings in their local small bank while dismissing an insurance carrier because it doesn't have pristine "A+" ratings. Have you ever walked into your local bank and asked them what their ratings were? Do you have any idea what their assets are or how their reserves work?

As a final point, I will leave you with this thought. As I mentioned above, there are more than four hundred banks that have failed since 2008. Many of them were small, local community banks. Can you guess how many "A"-rated insurance carriers failed during that same time frame? What about how many "B"-rated carriers? Can you guess how many "C"-rated insurance carriers failed during the same period? If you guessed zero to all three, you are correct.

Finally, with all the volatility in the stock market over the past ten years, we are 100 percent certain that every person reading this book either lost money themselves or knows countless people that did. Some of these people lost as much as 40 percent of their retirement savings. Well, we want to leave you with this thought. We have yet to meet or hear from a single consumer who has ever lost any money in one of these safe money retirement plans (fixed index annuities), assuming they played by the contract's rules and didn't surrender it early. In fact, we are willing to bet you have never met anyone who has either. Think how secure your retirement could have been if you had placed some of your retirement savings into one of these vehicles over the past ten years? The great news is that it is never too late to forge your own retirement destiny. And considering that this current economic volatility is likely to be around for some time, stop gambling your retirement away on the SS $401(k)$ and start looking for a more stable ship to get you to your final destination. You don't have to spend your retirement stressed out and worried that you'll be a burden to your children if you live longer than your retirement income.

Note: We always highly recommend speaking to a retirement income specialist about creating your own Safe Money Retirement plan. Keep in mind, most licensed insurance agents (including brokers, RIAs, and stock jockeys) can offer these. However, it is imperative that you speak to someone who truly understands them and has done a substantial amount of research and due diligence, as well as someone who has a history of happy clients with index annuities. We created a free website so that you can find retirement income specialists in your area. Go to www.annuity123.

com and click on "Annuity Harmony," where you will be taken to an interactive map.

Best of luck, and may all of your retirement dreams become reality.

Appendix

Employer-Sponsored Retirement Plans (continued from phase 3)

Many of today's larger employers offer retirement savings plans for their employees. These plans can provide a great way for workers to set aside funds for their future. Employer sponsors of retirement plans often offer incentives for participation such as providing matching contributions for employees in the plan.

The funds related to these retirement plans are also, oftentimes, tax advantaged in that they may go into the employees' accounts pretax and typically grow on a tax-deferred basis.

- **401(k) plan** – Certainly, one of the most popular employer-sponsored retirement plans today is the 401(k) plan. These plans allow employees of the sponsoring company to defer a certain percentage of their salary on a pretax basis into an account set up for that employee. (Although there are some cases where the employee may fund some contributions on an after-tax basis.) The funds in the account grow tax-deferred until they are withdrawn at the employee's retirement. Oftentimes, the employer that sponsors the plan will also make a percentage matching contribution to employees' accounts.

There are annual contribution limits set forth for employees who participate in 401(k) plans. In 2012, the maximum contribution that can be deferred into an individual's plan is $17,000, unless that employee is over the age of fifty. In this case, the employee may make an additional catch-up contribution of up to $5,500.

Upon retirement, the employee will be levied ordinary income tax against the funds withdrawn. If an individual who is under the age of 59½ withdraws funds from their plan, other than for a specific qualifying exception, they will incur an IRS penalty of 10 percent of the amount of funds withdrawn. This penalty is in addition to the income taxes due.

- **Money purchase plan** – Money purchase plans allow both an employee and the sponsoring employer to make contributions. These contributions are based primarily on a percentage of the employee's annual earnings.

When the employee reaches retirement, the funds in his or her account are used to purchase a lifetime annuity that will provide a stream of retirement income. An annual contribution limit is imposed on money purchase plans. For 2012, the contribution limit amount is 25 percent of the employee's total compensation, up to $50,000.

Similar to a 401(k) plan, funds contributed to a money purchase plan are done so on a pretax basis, and the funds are allowed to grow tax-deferred until the time of withdrawal. At that time, the plan participant is taxed at his or her ordinary income tax rate.

Also similar to a 401(k) plan, should funds be withdrawn by the participant prior to age 59½, other than for a qualifying exception, there is a 10 percent IRS penalty imposed on the amount of funds withdrawn.

- **Employee Stock Ownership Plan (ESOP)** – Employee Stock Ownership Plans are designed so that participants can invest specifically in the stock shares of the sponsoring employer. This, in essence, is done so for the purpose of benefitting the company's stock performance.

Some of the key benefits to participating in an ESOP plan are that the company stock contributions of cash and stock, as well as the dividends paid out from the stock, are all tax deductible.

As with most other retirement plans, there is an annual contribution limit imposed on ESOP plans. In 2012, this limit is 25 percent of an employee's eligible compensation. In addition, the combined contributions of both the employee and employer may not exceed 100 percent of the employee's annual compensation, up to a maximum of $50,000.

Should an ESOP participant leave the sponsoring employer, the individual is given their shares of company stock, and the company is required to purchase those stock shares back from the terminating employee at the stock's current fair market value. In addition, should a participating employee withdraw funds from an ESOP prior to turning age 59½, other than for a qualifying reason, they incur a 10 percent IRS penalty.

- **403(b) plan** – A 403(b) retirement plan is geared specifically to employees of public schools, certain ministers, and certain tax-exempt entities. With these plans, the employee's retirement account is allowed to invest either in mutual funds or annuities. For the most part, the workings of a 403(b) plan are similar to a 401(k) plan in that the participants may make contributions via salary deferral, up to a certain annual limit.

- **457(b) plan** – 457(b) retirement plans also have many similarities to 401(k) plans in that the participants can contribute into the plan via a salary deferral, and the employer can also make contributions to the employees' accounts. These types of retirement plans are primarily offered to state and local government employees such as firefighters, police officers, and certain public school workers, as well as to certain nongovernment organizations such as tax-exempt charities, hospital workers, and unions. A 457(b) plan also has annual contribution limits: $17,000 for 2012, with an additional $5,500 for those participants age fifty or older. In addition, 457(b) plans may allow for a "final three year" additional contribution for employees who are in the last three years of their employment prior to retiring. These contribution limits are in addition to the catch-up amounts allowed for employees fifty or older.

If an employee withdraws funds prior to reaching age 59½, other than for a qualifying reason, then they are assessed a 10 percent IRS penalty on the amount of funds withdrawn.

- **401(a) plan** – 401(a) retirement plans are a type of money purchase plan, yet, in many ways, they mirror a 401(k) plan. These plans are offered to employees of nonprofit organizations. As long as an employee works more than twenty hours per week with a total of one thousand hours and one year of service prior to joining, they are eligible to participate in such a plan.

There are several ways in which funds may be contributed to a 401(a) retirement plan. These include via employer contribution either with or without an employee contribution, an employer-matching amount based on the employee contribution, and/or an employer-matching amount within a given dollar-amount range.

These types of plans also have limits on the amount of annual contributions that can be made, as well as an IRS-imposed penalty for funds withdrawn from the plan prior to the employee reaching age 59½.

Self-Employed and Small Business Retirement Savings Plans

In addition to the plans that are allowed for larger companies, owners of small businesses and self-employed individuals are permitted to contribute to certain types of retirement savings plans. Some of these include the following:

- **SEP IRA** – A Simplified Employee Pension IRA, or SEP IRA, can be set up for either a self-employed individual or a small business owner. These plans are a variation of the IRA plan.

Similar to other retirement savings plans, there is an annual contribution limit for a SEP IRA. In 2012, this limit is 25 percent of the participant's annual compensation, up to a maximum of $50,000. These types of plans do not allow an additional amount of catch-up contribution for participants age fifty or over. Contributions to SEP IRA plans go in on a pretax basis. Therefore, when funds are withdrawn at retirement, the funds are taxed at the participant's then current income tax rate.

While inside the account, funds grow on a tax-deferred basis. Similar to other types of retirement savings plans, should a participant withdraw funds from the SEP IRA plan prior to reaching age 59½, other than for a qualifying reason, he or she will be penalized an additional 10 percent of the amount of the withdrawal.

- **SIMPLE IRA** – The term SIMPLE IRA stands for Savings Incentive Match Plans for Employees IRA. These types of retirement savings plans may be used by employers that have no more than one hundred employees. In addition, all eligible employees for a SIMPLE IRA plan must earn at least $5,000 annually, must have earned at least this amount for the past two years, and are expected to earn this much or more in the current year as well.

SIMPLE IRAs may also be set up for self-employed individuals. The tax treatment and other rules of the plan are similar to that of a SIMPLE IRA available to small businesses. The primary difference between the two is that a self-employed individual will fund both the employee and the employer portion of the contributions.

In 2012, SIMPLE IRA plans have an annual contribution limit of $17,000, as well as an additional allowable catch-up contribution of up to $2,500 for those employees age fifty and over. Contributions to a SIMPLE IRA go into the account on a pretax basis, and the funds inside of the account are allowed to grow tax-deferred. When the employee reaches retirement, withdrawals from a SIMPLE IRA will be taxed at the individual's then current income tax rate.

Similar to other types of retirement savings plans, there is a 10 percent IRS penalty imposed for non-qualifying withdrawals prior to the participant reaching age 59½. In addition, should a participant who is under age 59½ make a non-qualifying withdrawal from their SIMPLE IRA within two years of joining the plan, the IRS penalty will increase to 25 percent of the amount withdrawn.

- **SARSEP** – Salary Reduction Simplified Employee Pension Plans, or SARSEPs, allow employees of a small business to contribute to a retirement savings account with pretax funds. These types of plans are allowable for businesses that have twenty-five or fewer total employees. SARSEP plans have annual 2012 employee contribution limits of $17,000 or 25 percent of the employee's annual compensation, whichever amount is less. In addition, those employees age fifty and over may contribute an additional catch-up amount of $5,500.

Employers may also contribute to employees' SARSEP plans, with the maximum amount here being 25 percent of the employee's compensation (up to $50,000 in 2012). The funds inside of a SARSEP plan grow on a tax-deferred basis until withdrawn. Upon withdrawal, the participant's funds will be taxed at their then current income tax rate. And, as with other types of retirement plans, there will be an IRS penalty of 10 percent imposed on withdrawal amounts taken prior to the employee participant reaching the age of 59½.

- **Solo 401(k) plan** – Solo 401(k) retirement savings plans may be set up by those who are self-employed, however, those business owners who have a spouse who works as a full- or part-time employee of the business may also qualify to participate in a Solo 401(k) plan.

Like a regular 401(k) plan, a Solo 401(k) plan has annual contribution limits. For 2012, the participant may defer $17,000 into the account, and if they are age fifty or over, an additional $5,500 may also be contributed. There is a way, however, for participants of these plans to contribute an additional amount as profit sharing.

Also similar to a regular 401(k) plan, funds deferred into the plan go in pretax, are allowed to grow tax-deferred, and are taxed as ordinary income when withdrawn at retirement. A 10 percent

IRS early withdrawal penalty also applies to those funds withdrawn prior to the participant turning age 59½ (with just a few exceptions).

One distinguishing feature of a Solo 401(k) plan is that the participant may be allowed to use the balance in the account as collateral for a loan. In addition, similar to IRAs, Solo 401(k) plans have both a traditional and a Roth option.

Individual Retirement Savings Options–IRAs

Individuals may also set up retirement savings accounts—and in many cases, individual plans may be established even if the individual is also a participant in an employer-sponsored plan. (In these cases, the pretax status of certain contributions may be affected.)

One such plan is the Individual Retirement Account, or IRA. These types of plans may be set up as either a traditional IRA or a Roth IRA. Each have some distinguishing features, especially in terms of tax status when the funds are placed into the account as well as when they are withdrawn.

- **Traditional IRA** – Traditional IRA accounts allow their owners to save money on a pretax basis. The funds deposited into the account are also allowed to grow tax-deferred, being taxed as ordinary income when the participant withdraws the funds at retirement.

In order to set up a traditional IRA, an individual must qualify based on their age as well as their income status. Due to their tax-advantaged status, the IRS imposes contribution limits for these plans as well as a 10 percent penalty on early withdrawals.

In 2012, the maximum amount an IRA account holder may deposit is $5,000. These plans also allow an additional catch-up contribution of $1,000 for those age fifty or over on or before December 31 of the contribution year.

Owners of a traditional IRA are required to begin taking a minimum withdrawal amount when they reach age 70½, and failure to comply with this rule may subject the account holder to IRS penalties.

- **Roth IRA** – Roth IRAs work in a similar fashion to traditional IRAs, however, there are several key differences. One is that funds contributed to a Roth IRA are done so with after-tax dollars. This means that the deposited funds have already been taxed. In addition, the growth of the funds within an IRA is not subject to taxation and withdrawals are tax-free.

Like a traditional IRA, there are similar annual contribution limits and catch-up contributions with Roth IRAs. Yet, another primary difference between the two types of IRAs is that with a Roth IRA, the account holder is not required to begin withdrawing funds at any set age. Therefore, the funds within a Roth IRA account may be left in the account for an indefinite amount of time (or at least until the account owner passes away, at which time withdrawals are required to be made).

Characteristic	Traditional IRA	Roth IRA
Contributions	Contributions are made with *pre-tax dollars*. Earnings are tax-deferred, meaning you pay tax on withdrawal	Roth IRA contributions are made with *after-tax dollars*. But you pay no taxes at withdrawal.
Eligibility and Income Limits	<ul><li>You must have earned income equal to or greater than your contribution.</li><li>No maximum income limit.</li><li>You must be under age 70½</li><li>Nonworking spouse of a wage earner can also start an IRA if joint return is filed.</li></ul>	<ul><li>You must have earned income equal to or greater than your contribution.</li><li>No Age limit</li><li>Your modified adjusted gross income must fall within the limits prescribed by the IRS which are: *Married* : $167,000 - $176,000 *Single* : $105,000 - $120,000</li></ul>
Maximum Contribution	Contribution limited to $5,000 ($6,000 for employees 50 or over)	Contribution limited to $5,000 ($6,000 for employees 50 or over).
Distributions	Distributions must begin no later than age 70½, unless still working. 10% federal penalty tax on withdrawals before age 59½ unless an exception applies.	No requirement to start taking distributions while owner is alive. 10% federal penalty tax on withdrawals of **earnings** before age 59½ unless an exception applies.
Contribution deadline	April 15 of the following year for any given tax year.	April 15 of the following year for any given tax year.

Source: Google Images

Glossary

1035 Exchange: A tax-free transfer of an annuity contract from one insurer to another. A good reason to switch insurance companies is to lock in a higher return rate. Although a 1035 transfer is tax-free, it might be accompanied by a surrender charge if surrender fees have yet to lapse.

401(k) plan: A plan offered by an employer that lets employees make contributions to a retirement savings plan on a pre-tax basis, sometimes fully or partially matching these contributions.

403(b) plan: Similar to the 401(k) plan, but generally offered by nonprofit organizations instead of for-profit businesses. Allows contributions from employees to grow on a tax-deferred basis until they are withdrawn. At withdrawal, the funds are subject to tax like ordinary income.

457 Plan: Named in reference to the portion of the Internal Revenue Code that defines its basic rules, the 457 is a tax-exempt deferred compensation program provided to employees in state and federal governments and agencies. While similar to the 401(k) plan, the 457 plan never receives matching contributions from the employer, nor does the IRS consider it to be a qualified retirement plan.

A

Accrued Monthly Benefit (AMB): This is the monthly amount earned toward an employee's pension via that individual's service to the employing company.

Annuitant: The individual who receives payments from an annuity plan under the terms of that plan.

Annuity: Refers to the payments made on a periodic basis to an individual under an annuity plan. The payments are generally provided until the individual dies.

Actuary: The individual who uses statistical mathematics to calculate the premiums, dividends, reserves, and pension, insurance and annuity rates for an insurance company or other institution involved with fiscal risk.

Adjusted Gross Income (AGI): The amount of income obtained after subtracting allowable adjustments from the total income received. These adjustments include contributions to an IRA, paid alimony, moving expenses, and contributions to Keogh accounts.

After-Tax Dollars: Refers to the amount of money remaining after taxes have been paid on it. See also Non-Qualified Annuity

Anniversary Date: The anniversary of the date on which an annuity starts or becomes effective. Index annuities calculate annual yield by taking the difference in the S&P 500 between anniversary dates.

Annual Reset: A way of calculating annual yield for an index annuity in which the baseline from which growth is measured resets every year. With an annual reset, previous years' growth is never lost and you lock in your gains each and every year.

Annuitant: The individual whose life expectancy is used to determine the term of income payments to be made under an annuity contract; generally, but not necessarily, the person who receives this income. The annuitant cannot make premium deposits or cancel the contract, and has no say over the terms of the annuity or when to withdraw money. The annuitant must typically sign the contract.

Annuitant-Driven: Annuity contracts with provisions that trigger upon the death of a designated individual (annuitant). Besides death, an annuitant's reaching of a certain age or becoming disabled, can trigger contract provisions.

Annuitization: The process of converting an annuity contract's value into an income stream represented by periodic payments made over a specified period of time.

Annuity: A plan that allows individuals to make tax-deferred contributions to a retirement savings account and to select a payout option that meets their income needs upon retirement.

Annuity Certain: An immediate annuity (SPIA) income plan from which payments are made for a defined period of time, whether or not the annuitant lives or dies.

Annuity Contract: A legal contract in which an insurer promises to make periodic payments to a designated individual over a specific period of time beginning on a set date in exchange for that individual's payment of premiums to the insurer.

Annuity Period: The length of time between income payments made under an annuity income plan; the time span may be monthly, quarterly, semi-annually, or annually.

Assumed Investment Rate: The minimum rate of interest that must be obtained on investments in a variable annuity in order to cover the costs and expected profits of an insurance company.

B

Bailout Provision: A provision in an annuity contract that allows the owner to surrender the contract, generally without charge, if the renewal interest rates on a fixed annuity drop under the pre-determined amount (usually 1%).

Basis Point: A unit of measure, with 100 basis points being equal to one percentage point.

Before-Tax Dollars: Amounts of money that have not been subjected to taxation. See also Qualified Annuity.

Beneficiary: The individual or legal entity receiving an annuity death benefit when the annuitate designated in the contract dies. Typically a child or spouse. The beneficiary cannot manage the annuity -- a right reserved solely for the contract owner.

Bond: A form of debt created by an institution that wants to borrow money. Buyers of bonds receive periodic payments of interest, with the principal amount of the bond typically repaid as a lump sum by a specified date.

Bonus Annuity: The amount added by an insurance company to the premium payments of fixed, deferred annuities with surrender charges. Usually imposed as additional interest or principal in the contract's first year and usually totals between 1% to 10%.

C

Cafeteria Plan: An employee benefit plan that provides flexible dollars to be used by employees to pay for specific benefits from a list of choices, such as life insurance or health insurance, to put into a 401(k) plan or to use instead of a 401(k).

Catch-Up Provision: With this provision, employees with 403(b) plans can contribute more than is usually allowed to their plans.

Certificate Annuity: A type of annuity in which the interest rate guarantee period is equal to the surrender charge period.

Certificate of Deposit (CD): Certificates issued by banks in exchange for a cash deposit, which is held for a certain period of time and a set interest rate. A bank pays the CD holder the principal amount and all accumulated interest once the specified time period is over.

Charitable Gift Annuity: An annuity in which a donor provides property to a charity in exchange for an income.

Cliff Vesting: A vesting schedule by which employees may not receive any part of a retirement benefit until "fully vested," or under a predetermined number of years of service to the employing organization.

Co-Annuitant (or Joint Annuitant): Second individual whose life determines the length of an annuity contract. Seldom indicated, the co-annuitant typically prolongs a contract because both annuitant and co-annuitant must die for the term to cease.

Collateral: Certain property provided by an individual seeking a loan as security for repaying the loan amount.

Compound Interest: Interest on money that accrues on both principal and accumulated interest.

Confinement Waiver: An arrangement in which surrender charges are eliminated if the annuity owner must be cared for in a hospital or long-term care facility due to medical necessity.

Consumer Price Index (CPI): The percent change in costs of consumer goods and services. CPI is a metric of consumer-felt inflation, measuring how far your dollar goes towards buying common goods and services. Typically rises 1-3% per year.

Contract Owner: The person or entity that makes application for and buys an annuity contract. This party is responsible for funding the annuity. An owner could be an individual, couple, partnership, corporation, or trust.

Contract Termination: The forced end to an annuity due to death of the annuitant.

Contract Value: The total of paid premiums and earnings, less any charges, withdrawals, or fees that may apply.

Custodian: The institution or individual holding the assets of another. For example, a custodian may be a bank that holds the assets of a corporation or mutual fund, or it may be an adult who is responsible for the financial activities of a minor child.

D

Death Benefit: The annuity benefit paid to a designated beneficiary when the annuity contract's owner dies.

Debt Instruments: Investments involving the lending of money, where returns are made by charging interest. CDs, treasuries, government bonds, loans, and promissory notes are all debt instruments that promise to return principle plus interest at a future date.

Deferred Annuity: An annuity that provides a way to accumulate monies tax-deferred. Usually meaning income is not going to be utilized immediately.

Deferred Compensation: Compensation for services rendered provided under an agreement stating that such compensation will be paid sometime in the future, after the actual services have been performed.

Defined Debit Plan: A pension plan in which a lifetime retirement income is guaranteed on the basis of employee income and/or total years of service to the employer.

Defined Contribution Plan: A pension plan whereby an employer deposits a yearly contribution into the plan for each of the plan's participants, with retirement income depending on these contributed amounts.

Discretionary Income: The amount of money from income that remains after an individual pays essential bills, such as food, housing, and taxes.

Disposition: Ability to distribute fund pending the termination of an annuity.

Diversification: The allocation of assets to several different types of investments so as to reduce the risks associated with any single investment, the idea being that losses in one area would be offset by gains in another.

Duration: Timeframe of an annuity contract: 1, 2, 3, 5, 7, or 10 years. The longer the duration, the better the return rate on fixed annuities.

E

Employee Retirement Income Security Act (ERISA): The federal law that formed the basis for modern pension regulation by establishing requirements for nondiscrimination, vesting, participation, reporting and disclosure, as well as standards for funding and fiduciary responsibilities.

Endorsement: An addition written to an insurance policy that includes provisions superseding those of the original policy. It is also known as a rider.

Endowment: An insurance policy that pays out its face amount to the individual insured when it reaches maturity, if that person is still alive. If the insured has died before the policy matures, the face amount is paid to a designated beneficiary.

Equity Indexed Annuity (see also Fixed Indexed Annuity): A type of fixed annuity that earns interest connected to an outside equity index, such as the S&P 500 (Standard & Poor's 500 Composite Stock Price Index).

Equity Vehicle: Investments involving ownership of company stock, futures, commodities, or real estate. Profit in equity vehicles results from their sale after appreciation (growth in value).

Estate Planning: Refers to the preparations made for the administration and disposition of an individual's property either before or after his or her death. Plans may include the creation of wills, trusts, and gifts.

Exclusion Ratio: A calculation used to calculate the taxable and non-taxable parts of each payment to an annuitant from an immediate annuity. Part of each payment is considered a return of principal and therefore not subject to taxation, while the remainder includes earnings on interest, which are taxable.

Executor: An individual named in a will who is designated to carry out the wishes of the deceased person for the distribution of his or her property and who performs this activity under the supervision of a court.

F

Fiduciary: An individual or organization that exercises control over a pension plan and/or the assets it holds.

Fixed Annuity (can also be known as MYGA – Multi-year Guarantee Annuity): An annuity contract that provides a guaranteed minimum interest rate and a higher current interest rate for shorter time periods during a deferred annuity's accumulation phase.

Fixed Indexed Annuity (see also Equity Indexed Annuity): A type of fixed annuity that earns interest connected to an outside equity index, such as the S&P 500 (Standard & Poor's 500 Composite Stock Price Index).

Flat-Rate Premium: Refers to the premium rate paid on a yearly basis by pension plans to the Pension Benefit Guaranty Corporate (PBGC) on behalf of each plan participant. The rates for multi-employer and single-employer plans are different.

Flexible Premium: A kind of annuity that may be bought into multiple times in the future. After depositing the initial premium, further investment can be made into the same annuity.

Flexible Premium Deferred Annuity (FPDA): A type of annuity in which the owner has the option to invest more money in the future, and which forgoes periodic payouts in favor of compounding interest.

Forced Annuitization: The mandatory liquidation of an annuity and dispersion of funds, triggered by the death the annuitant, or if the annuitant reaches certain maximum age.

Forfeiture: The amount lost when a pension plan participant leaves the employing organization before becoming fully vested under the plan's schedule.

Free Look Provision: The provision in an annuity contract stating that the owner of the contract has between ten and 20 days to review the contract immediately after buying it. It gives the buyer the chance to return the contract to the insurer for a total refund and is governed by state regulations, which may vary.

Free Withdrawal Provision: The provision in an annuity contract that allows the owner to withdraw some part of its face value, without the imposition of a withdrawal charge, during the accumulation period.

Frozen Plan: A qualified retirement plan that disallows the continuing benefits accruals of or additional contributions for current employees and also does not permit the recognition of new plan participants.

Fully Funded: When a pension plan has enough assets to pay for all of its current benefits and those promised for the future, it is said to be fully funded.

G

Guaranteed Interest Rate: The minimum interest rate an insurer will credit during an annuity contract's accumulation phase, usually between three and four percent.

Guaranteed Minimum Surrender Value: Index annuities are regulated by the National Association of Insurance Commissioners, which requires investors to at least receive 90% principle + 3% for every year the contract was held.

H

Holding Period: The period of time during which an investor has ownership of a capital asset.

I

Immediate Annuity (also known as SPIA): An annuity contract that begins its payout immediately or within a year.

Income or Payout Options: Refer to the various ways the owner of an annuity contract may receive income from an immediate annuity.

Index: A statistical system that measures and tracks the performance of similar investments as a group such as the S&P 500.

Individual Retirement Account (IRA): A retirement program that permits individuals who have earned income to save part of that income in a tax-deferred savings plan. IRAs can be created and funded any time between the first day of the current year up to and including the date on which individual income tax returns are due, usually April 15 of the following year.

Initial Interest Rate: The rate of interest that is applied to the first deposit made to a fixed, deferred annuity, with the length of time this rate is guaranteed specified in the annuity contract

Insurer (the insurance company): One of the four parties to any annuity contract. The insurer is the company to whom the owner pays the premium. The insurer invests the premium and doles out payments.

Interest: Fees paid by banks, entities that issue bonds, and other financial institutions for the use of money provided on loan.

J

Joint Annuitant: A person named in an annuity contract in addition to the owner. This person's age and life expectancy are used along with those of the contract owner to calculate the amount of annuity payments.

Joint Life Annuity: A type of annuity that continues to provide payments to a spouse after the death of the contract owner, regardless of the date of the death. It also allows for the designation of additional beneficiaries if the spouse dies.

Joint Owner: An individual who co-owns an annuity contract with another person. Both have the right to make and approve decisions relating to the contract.

K

L

Life Annuity: An annuity that pays a set amount on a regular, periodic basis, for the duration of the annuitant's life.

Liquidity: The ability to quickly convert assets into cash by an individual or organization without incurring significant losses of value.

Load: The sales fee or charge imposed on the owner who buys an annuity contract.

M

Market Value Adjustment (MVA): A kind of fixed annuity in which there is a guaranteed rate unless the contract owner withdraws amounts that exceed a specific free-withdrawal amount, or if the owner terminates the annuity contract before it matures.

Maturity Date: The date on which an annuity starts to make income payouts.

Money Market: Refers to the market for very liquid and low-risk short-term assets, including Treasury bills and negotiable Certificates of Deposit.

Multiple Premium Annuity: This is an annuity program that requires more than one premium payment.

Mutual Fund: An account combining the funds of many individuals in order to invest these funds in a range of financial instruments. A financial service company usually establishes this type of account.

N

Net Worth: The difference between the total value of an individual's assets and the total of all of his or her liabilities.

Non-Qualified Annuity: Non-qualified refers to the part of an annuity plan that can be attributed to the return of capital and is therefore not subject to taxation; the interest portion is taxable, however.

O

Owner-Driven: An Annuity whose provisions trigger upon the death, reaching of a certain age, or disability of the contract owner.

P

Participation Rate: Also call the Index Rate, this refers to the part of the index's increase credited to an equity-indexed annuity's account value. In some contracts, a cap is imposed on this amount.

Payout Period: The period of time during which an annuitant is provided payments from an immediate annuity plan.

Payout Ratio: A calculation in an annuity income rider that determines the percentage that your income account will be multiplied by. Usually based on age, and in the 4% – 8% range.

Pension Plan: A qualified plan designed to provide payments to an employee upon retirement. Pension plans comprise a yearly funding commitment from employers, no access to plan funds before retirement, and restrictions on investments in employer stock to ten percent.

Period Certain: An income option in an immediate annuity plan whereby the owner of the annuity contract may choose to receive periodic payments for a set period of time, with the payout amount determined by the contract's value and the length of the period of time chosen.

Point-to-Point: A way of calculating index annuity yield. The total yield is simply the difference in index value from the day the annuity is purchased to the day it expires.

Portfolio: A group of investments considered a unit.

Premature Distributions: The withdrawal of earnings amounts from an annuity program before the annuity contract's owner reaches 59.5 years of age. Usually accompanied by a 10% penalty from the IRS.

Premium Bonus: Additional funds that are credited by an insurer to an annuity, expressed as a percentage of the deposited amount.

Premium Tax: Refers to a separate tax imposed on premiums for life insurance or an annuity plan by state governments. While not all states impose this tax, those that do may have different regulations for qualified and non-qualified programs.

Prescribed Annuity: Prescribed Annuity Contracts (PACs) offer non-taxable returns on investment, and the annuitant's interest income is included at a steady rate during the entire term of the annuity. The amount taxed is lower than that in a non-prescribed annuity early in the term, but rises later on.

Principal: The total amount of money that an annuity contract owner has put into the annuity, excluding earned interest.

Private Annuity: Refers to a contract entered into by two people who agree to exchange a valuable asset for payment of income for the duration of life.

Prospectus: A written document that must be provided under federal regulations to the prospective buyer of a variable annuity before the actual sale. The document describes the investment goals of accounts, past performance of any sub-accounts included, and defines fees and other expenses.

Q

Qualified Annuity: A type of annuity bought with the intention to fund or distribute money from a tax-qualified plan, generally with paid premiums reducing current income tax and the use of tax-deferred accumulations. (for example, IRA's, 401(k)'s, and SEP's are all Qualified plans.)

R

Renewal Rate: The new rate of interest credited to an annuity after the current interest-rate period is over, typically on the anniversary of the contract. This rate may be higher or lower than the current rate, depending on economic conditions and the investments used by the insurer.

Risk-Return Trade-Off: A way of comparing the risks and returns of a potential investment by considering the age of the investor and the time frame for the investment, with higher risks generating greater returns.

Rollover: Refers to the monies from a qualified retirement plan or IRA (Individual Retirement Account) that are shifted from one plan to another plan of the same kind, maintaining the tax-deferred status of the funds.

Roth IRA: While similar to a traditional IRA (Individual Retirement Account), the Roth IRA's contributions are not deductible. Account distributions may be obtained free of federal income tax if certain conditions are met, however.

S

Simplified Employee Pension (SEP): A type of retirement plan in which an IRA (Individual Retirement Account) is used to hold contributions; a simpler alternative to a 401(k) or profit-sharing plan.

Single-Employer Plan: A type of pension plan that is sponsored by one employer or a group of employers under a common control structure. It may also be a pension program that is not collectively bargained and is sponsored by a group of unrelated firms.

Single Life Annuity: A type of annuity plan in which the periodic payments are made to the annuity contract owner for life, but end after the owner dies.

Single Premium: A kind of annuity into which funds cannot be deposits after the initial investment. Fixed-rate annuities are commonly of this type, requiring a second annuity purchase should the contract owner decide to invest more money at a future date.

Single Premium Deferred Annuity (SPDA): A kind of annuity that may be bought into once and whose payouts are withheld, compounding interest. Future investments require a new annuity purchase.

Single Premium Immediate Annuity (SPIA): A kind of annuity that may be bought into once and yields periodic payouts (monthly, quarterly, or annually) at the cost of compound interest. Future investments require a new annuity purchase.

Split-Funded Annuity: An annuity contract in which the plan's owner divides the initial premium into two separate contracts, with one portion of the premium deposit going to a fixed deferred annuity with a guaranteed interest rate over a set period of time, and the other portion going to an immediate annuity that pays income during the same time period.

Standard Termination: Refers to the termination of a plan that holds assets sufficient to pay all benefits.

Straight Life Annuity: A type of annuity plan paying a specified amount over a set period of time until the death of the annuitant. There are no payouts available to survivors after the contract owner dies.

Substandard Health Annuity: A type of straight-life annuity designed for individuals who have serious health problems. The cost of this annuity depends on the life expectancy of the annuitant, with lower life expectancies being more expensive, since the insurer has less of a chance to obtain a profit from the investor's funds. The periodic payouts are much higher to persons with low life expectancies, however.

Sub-Account: Portion of a variable annuity allocating investment into a specific segment, like a money market account, the S&P 500, mutual funds, or Pacific Basin stocks. The choice of sub-accounts makes up the variable annuity portfolio.

Surrender Charge: A penalty imposed by the insurer if the contract owner terminates the annuity prematurely, by withdrawing all funds.

Surrender Value: Refers to the amount of money received by a contract owner if the annuity is surrendered and all cash is taken out of it.

Surviving Spouse: The term used to describe the living spouse of a deceased plan participant. Under a Qualified Domestic Relations Order (QDRO), a former spouse may be considered a surviving spouse.

T

Tax-Deductible: An amount of money deducted from the adjusted gross income of a taxpayer in order to calculate the total of taxable income. Medical expenses, paid mortgage interest, and charitable contributions itemized on Schedule A of federal income forms are examples of tax-deductible expenses.

Tax-Deferral: Refers to the fact that earnings from an annuity are not taxed until they are withdrawn from the plan.

Transfers: An activity whereby owners of Qualified contract may move assets from one plan to an annuity without the imposition of tax liability on these funds.

Tax-Sheltered Annuity (TSA): A type of retirement annuity available for purchase only by public school teachers and individuals employed by colleges, hospitals and other entities that offer qualified retirement programs under Internal Revenue Code Section 403(b).

Temporary Annuity: A type of life annuity that is set to expire after the passing of a pre-established period of time.

Term Certain Annuity: A kind of annuity plan in which pre-defined income payments are provided until the expiration date of the annuity product. Payments are typically made on a monthly basis for the term of the contract. If the expiry date occurs before the annuitant dies, however, that individual no longer receives a steady income stream.

Treasuries: A term that refers to all of the federal government's negotiable securities. Treasury bills (T-bills) have short-term maturities of three and six months and do not pay interest. Instead, they are sold at face value. Treasury bonds may be obtained in $1,000 units and have maturities of ten years or more. Treasury notes have medium-term maturities of between one and ten years.

Trustee: The individual or organization charged with receiving, managing, and distributing plan assets.

Two-Tier Annuity: A type of annuity that is designed to have a high interest rate, compared to the market, during its first year, based on the assumption that the owner of the annuity contract will remain in the plan through the annuitization period.

U

V

Variable Annuity: A kind of annuity contract that allows the owner to allocate the premium amount among several investments, or sub-accounts. The contract value of such a plan may vary according to the performance of these investments.

Vesting: The term used to describe an employee's gaining of the right to be paid a current or future benefit from a pension plan.

W

Withdrawal Charge: A penalty imposed by the insurer if the contract owner cashes out part of the annuity prematurely. Withdrawal charges typically phase out according to a schedule, e.g., 10% before 3 year, 5% after 4 years, 0% after 5 years. Withdrawal charges may be waived in the event of death or illness.

X

Y

Yield:
capital investment. Also the income portion of the return from a security.

Z

About the Authors

Joe Simonds is the founder of Annuity Think Tank, an independent educational, research, and retirement marketing group specializing in annuities and retirement income. In the past ten years, he has consulted with and assisted financial professionals in writing in excess of $1 billion in annuity production. Joe has had the opportunity to consult more than one thousand agents in growing their practice and has been responsible for helping multiple producers expand their annuity business from $10 million to over $25 million. He has flown all over the country to assist advisors in educating clients on retirement income and has been a guest host on radio shows as well.

Joe is originally a native of Florida. He moved to Atlanta to attend Georgia Tech, where he graduated with highest honors, earning a bachelor's degree in Business Management. He also received a minor in both Finance and Economics.

Joe is married to his lovely wife, Loren, and they currently reside in Houston, Texas, with their daughter Shauna Taylor. They enjoy traveling and any activity where a boat or water is involved.

Nathan Lee began his career in the financial services industry more than ten years ago as an independent financial advisor. He has held both series 6 and 63 licenses and has endeavored to provide his clients with the most tax-advantaged retirement solutions. After a break from the financial services industry, Nathan returned as a top recruiter for one of the industry's largest marketing firms. He then joined Annuity Think Tank as a marketing consultant and recently accepted the position of chief marketing officer. He has been tasked with the continued development of value-added programs designed to expand his clients' practices and make them more profitable.

Nathan is a true Atlanta, Georgia, native and received a bachelor's degree in Business Management from Georgia Tech with minors in Corporate Finance and Regional and Economic Real Estate Development. When not at the office, Nathan enjoys adventure races, mud runs, riding his motorcycle, and other outdoor sports.

Franco Devivo began his career as a sales coach in the retirement planning industry in 2005. In 2007, he took the opportunity to move overseas for three years to work as a cash-flow analyst for one of the world's largest banks. Franco currently resides in Atlanta, Georgia, with his wife, Natalia, and daughters, Isabella and Alexa.

Jason Edward Chaifetz grew up in Marietta, Georgia, and earned an engineering degree from Georgia Tech. After college, Jason entered the insurance and annuity industry and helped grow a national annuity distribution firm to more than $1 billion in annual sales. After five years with that firm, Jason joined forces with Joe Simonds to start the Annuity Think Tank in 2009. He currently lives in Atlanta, Georgia, and spends his spare time playing soccer and traveling.

James Cline has been providing invaluable assistance and a very unique perspective to successful advisors and clients nationwide. His depth of experience is truly impressive, having served on both the wholesale and retail sides of the financial service industry for many years. Jamie is from South Georgia and played in the 2001 Baseball College World Series for the University of Georgia. Jamie spends his spare time hunting, fishing, and playing competitive softball.

Made in the USA
Charleston, SC
05 October 2012